ANCIENT STORIES OF A GREAT FLOOD

THE HUXLEY MEMORIAL LECTURE FOR 1916

SIR JAMES GEORGE FRAZER

COACHWHIP PUBLICATIONS

Greenville, Ohio

Ancient Stories of a Great Flood, by Sir James George Frazer
Facsimile reprint. First published 1916.
Journal of the Royal Anthropological Institute 46: 231-283.
© 2013 Coachwhip Publications
Cover: Ocean (CC) George Lenard
No claims made on public domain material.

CoachwhipBooks.com

ISBN 1-61646-171-3
ISBN-13 978-1-61646-171-3

ANCIENT STORIES OF A GREAT FLOOD.

The Huxley Memorial Lecture for 1916.

By Sir James George Frazer.

§1. Introduction.

When the Council of the Royal Anthropological Institute invited me to deliver the annual Huxley Lecture, I gratefully accepted the invitation, esteeming it a high honour to be thus associated with one for whom, both as a thinker and a man, I entertain a deep respect, and with whose attitude towards the great problems of life I am in cordial sympathy. His own works will long keep his memory green; but it is fitting that our science should lay, year by year, a wreath on the grave of one of the most honoured of its exponents.

Casting about for a suitable subject on which to address you, I remembered that in his later life Huxley devoted some of his well-earned leisure to examining those traditions as to the early ages of the world which are recorded in the Book of Genesis; and accordingly I thought that I might appropriately take one of them for the theme of my discourse. The one which I have chosen is the familiar story of the Great Flood. Huxley himself discussed it in an instructive essay written with all the charm of his lucid and incisive style.[1] His aim was to show that, treated as a record of a deluge which overwhelmed the whole world, drowning almost all men and animals, the story conflicts with the plain teaching of geology, and must be rejected as a fable. I shall not attempt either to reinforce or to criticize his arguments and his conclusions, for the simple reason that I am no geologist, and that for me to express an opinion on such a matter would be a mere impertinence. I have approached the subject from a different side, namely, from that of tradition. It has long been known that legends of a great flood, in which almost all men perished, are widely diffused over the world; and accordingly what I have tried to do is to collect and compare these legends, and to inquire what conclusions are to be deduced from the comparison. In short, my discussion of the stories is a study in comparative folk-lore. My purpose is to discover how the narratives arose and how they came to be so widespread over the earth; with the question of their truth or falsehood I am not primarily concerned, though, of course, it cannot be ignored in considering the problem of their origin. The inquiry thus defined is not a novel one. It has often been attempted, especially in

---

[1] "Hasisadra's Adventure," *Collected Essays*, vol. iv (London, 1911), pp. 239–296.

recent years, and in pursuing it I have made abundant use of the labours of my predecessors, some of whom have discussed the subject with great learning and ability. In particular I would acknowledge my debt to the eminent German geographer and anthropologist, the late Dr. Richard Andree, whose monograph on diluvial traditions, like all his writings, is a model of sound learning and good sense, set forth with the utmost clearness and conciseness.[1]

But the theme of deluge legends is too large to be treated of adequately within the compass of a single lecture, and instead of attempting to give you a comprehensive view of the whole subject, which would be apt to degenerate into a mere catalogue of legends and a bare statement of conclusions without the evidence on which they are based, I propose to confine our attention this evening to a few conspicuous instances of diluvial traditions and to handle these somewhat fully, believing that this mode of treatment is likely to prove more interesting to my hearers and to furnish them with more ample means of testing the value of my conclusions. The particular traditions which I have selected for discussion are the most famous and the most familiar of all, namely, the stories of a great flood which are recorded in the ancient literatures of Babylonia, Palestine, and Greece. What I have to say about similar tales discovered in other parts of the world must be reserved for another time and another place. But before I address myself to the particular legends to which I have the honour of inviting your attention to-night, permit me to make a single general observation on the study of diluvial traditions as a whole.

Apart from the intrinsic interest of such legends as professed records of a catastrophe which destroyed at a blow almost the whole human race, they deserve to be studied for the sake of their bearing on a general question which is at present warmly debated among anthropologists. That question is, How are we to explain the numerous and striking similarities which obtain between the beliefs and customs of races inhabiting distant parts of the world ? Are such resemblances due to the transmission of the customs and beliefs from one race to another, either

---

[1] R. Andree, *Die Flutsagen* (Brunswick, 1891). Other notable discussions of the same theme in recent years are the following : H. Usener, *Die Sintflutsagen* (Bonn, 1899) ; *id.*, "Zu den Sintfluthsagen," *Kleine Schriften*, iv (Berlin, 1913), pp. 382–396 ; M. Winternitz, *Die Flutsagen des Alterthums und der Naturvölker* (Vienna, 1901) (reprinted from *Mittheilungen der anthropologischen Gesellschaft in Wien*, vol. xxxi) ; E. Böklen, "Die Sintflutsage, Versuch einer neuen Erklärung," *Archiv für Religionswissenschaft*, vi (1903), pp. 1–61, 97–150 ; G. Gerland, *Der Mythus von der Sintflut* (Bonn, 1912). Of these works, that of Winternitz contains a useful list of flood legends, with references to the authorities and a full analysis of the principal incidents in the legends. Like the treatise of R. Andree, it is characterized by the union of accurate learning and good sense. On the other hand, the works of Usener, Böklen, and Gerland are vitiated by their far-fetched and improbable theories as to the origin of the legends in solar or lunar myths. But in spite of this defect, Gerland's treatise is valuable for the number of parallel legends which the author's ethnological learning has collected from many races. Among earlier discussions of the same theme may be mentioned Philipp Buttmann, "Ueber den Mythos der Sündflut," *Mythologus* (Berlin, 1828–1829), i, 180–214 ; François Lenormant, *Les Origines de l'Histoire d'après la Bible, de la Création de l'Homme au Déluge* (Paris, 1880), pp. 382–491.

through immediate contact or through the medium of intervening peoples? Or have they arisen independently in many different races through the similar working of the human mind under similar circumstances? Now, if I may presume to offer an opinion on this much-debated problem, I would say at once that, put in the form of an antithesis between mutually exclusive views, the question seems to me absurd. So far as I can judge, all experience and all probability are in favour of the conclusion that both causes have operated extensively and powerfully to produce the observed similarities of custom and belief among the various races of mankind; in other words, many of these resemblances are to be explained by simple transmission, with more or less of modification, from people to people, and many are to be explained as having originated independently through the similar action of the human mind in response to similar environment. If that is so—and I confess to thinking that this is the only reasonable and probable view—it will follow that in attempting to account for any particular case of resemblance which may be traced between the customs and beliefs of different races, it would be futile to appeal to the general principle either of transmission or of independent origin; each case must be judged on its own merits after an impartial scrutiny of the facts, and referred to the one or the other principle, or possibly to a combination of the two, according as the balance of evidence inclines to the one side or to the other, or hangs evenly between them.

Now this general conclusion, which accepts the two principles of transmission and independent origin as both of them true and valid within certain limits, is confirmed by the particular investigation of diluvial traditions. For it is certain that legends of a great flood are found dispersed among many diverse peoples in distant regions of the earth, and so far as demonstration in such matters is possible, it can be demonstrated that the similarities which undoubtedly exist between many of these legends are partly due to direct transmission from one people to another, and partly to similar, but quite independent, experiences either of great floods or of phenomena which suggested the occurrence of great floods, in many different parts of the world. Thus the study of these traditions, quite apart from any conclusions to which it may lead us concerning their historical credibility, may serve a useful purpose if it mitigates the heat with which the controversy has sometimes been carried on, by convincing the extreme partisans of both principles that in this, as in so many other disputes, the truth lies wholly neither on the one side nor on the other, but somewhere between the two.

So much for the study of flood stories in general. I now turn to the particular consideration of the flood stories current in sacred and classical antiquity.

§2. The Babylonian Story of a Great Flood.

Of all the legends of a great flood recorded in literature, by far the oldest is the Babylonian, or, rather, the Sumerian; for we now know that, ancient as was the Babylonian version of the story, it was derived by the Babylonians from their still more ancient predecessors, the Sumerians, from whom the Semitic inhabitants of Babylonia appear to have derived the principal elements of their civilization.

The Babylonian tradition of the Great Flood has been known to Western scholars from the time of antiquity, since it was recorded by the native historian Berosus, who composed a history of his country in the first half of the third century before our era. Berosus wrote in Greek, and his work has not come down to us, but fragments of it have been preserved by later Greek historians, and among these fragments is, fortunately, his account of the Deluge. It runs as follows :—[1]

"The Great Flood took place in the reign of Xisuthrus, the tenth king of Babylon. Now the god Cronus appeared to him in a dream and warned him that all men would be destroyed by a flood on the fifteenth day of the month Daesius, which was the eighth month of the Macedonian calendar.[2] Therefore the god enjoined him to write a history of the world from the beginning and to bury it for safety in Sippar, the city of the Sun.[3] Moreover, he was to build a ship and embark in it with his kinsfolk and friends, and to lay up in it a store of meat and drink, and to bring living things, both fowls and four-footed beasts, into the ship,

---

[1] Eusebius, *Chronicorum Liber Prior*, ed. A. Schoene (Berlin, 1875), coll. 19 *sqq.; Fragmenta Historicorum Graecorum*, ed. C. Müller, ii (Paris, 1878), pp. 501 *sq.* Eusebius had not the original work of Berosus before him. He copied from Julius Africanus, who copied from Alexander Polyhistor (a contemporary of Sulla in the first century B.C.), who copied from Apollodorus, who may have copied from Berosus himself. See C. Müller, *Fragmenta Historicorum Graecorum*, ii, 496. Even the original Greek text of Eusebius is lost and is known only through an Armenian translation, of which a Latin version is printed by A. Schoene and C. Müller, *ll.cc.* A Greek version of the Babylonian legend is preserved in the chronicle of the Christian writer, Georgius Syncellus, who lived at the end of the eighth and the beginning of the ninth century. The Greek version of Syncellus is printed side by side with the Latin translation of Eusebius's version in A. Schoene's edition of Eusebius's *Chronicle* and in C. Müller's *Fragmenta Historicorum Graecorum, ll.cc.*

[2] L. Ideler, *Handbuch der mathematischen und technischen Chronologie* (Berlin, 1825), i, 393, 402 *sq.;* W. Smith, *Dictionary of Greek and Roman Antiquities*, third edition (London, 1890–1891), i, 338 *sq., s.v.* "Calendar." The date is probably derived from Berosus himself, who, writing in Greek under the Macedonian empire, would naturally use the Macedonian calendar. However, we cannot say at what time of the year the month Daesius fell at Babylon in the time of Berosus, and consequently we do not know at what time of the year he supposed the Deluge to have occurred. For though the *order* of the months in the Macedonian calendar was the same everywhere, their *dates* fell differently in different places. See *The Dying God*, p. 116, note[1]. In one passage (*Aratus* 53) Plutarch tells us that the Macedonian month Daesius was equivalent to the Attic month Anthesterion, which roughly corresponded to our February. But elsewhere he says that the battle of Granicus was fought in the Macedonian month Daesius (*Alexander*, 16) and the Attic month Thargelion (*Camillus*, 19), which was approximately equivalent to our May.

[3] Κελεῦσαι οὖν διὰ γραμμάτων πάντων ἀρχὰς καὶ μέσα καὶ τελευτὰς ὀρύξαντα θεῖναι ἐν πόλει ἡλίου Σιππάροις. The Greek is peculiar and ambiguous. ὀρύξαντα, "having dug," might mean either that he was to bury the record in the ground or to dig it up. The corresponding word in the Armenian version of Eusebius is said to be equally ambiguous. I have preferred the former sense as more appropriate and as confirmed by the sequel (see below, p. 235). Σιππάροις is a correction of Scaliger for the manuscript reading Σισπάροις. In modern times many thousands of clay tablets containing records of legal transactions have been found in the ancient Babylonian city of Sippar. See Morris Jastrow, *The Religion of Babylonia and Assyria* (Boston, 1898), p. 10.

and when he had made all things ready he was to set sail. And when he asked, 'And whither shall I sail?' the god answered him, 'To the gods; but first thou shalt pray for all good things to men.' So he obeyed and built the ship, and the length of it was five furlongs,[1] and the breadth of it was two furlongs; and when he had gathered all things together he stored them in the ship and embarked his children and friends. And when the flood had come and immediately abated, Xisuthrus let fly some of the birds. But as they could find no food nor yet a place to rest, they came back to the ship. And again, after some days, Xisuthrus let fly the birds; and they returned again to the ship with their feet daubed with clay. A third time he let them fly, and they returned no more to the vessel. Then Xisuthrus perceived that the land had appeared above the water; so he parted some of the seams of the ship, and looking out he saw the shore, and drove the ship aground on a mountain, and stepped ashore with his wife, and his daughter, and the helmsman. And he worshipped the ground, and built an altar; and when he had sacrificed to the gods, he disappeared with those who had disembarked from the ship. And when those who had remained in the ship saw that he and his company returned not, they disembarked likewise and sought him, calling him by name. But Xisuthrus himself was nowhere to be seen. Yet a voice from the air bade them fear the gods, for that he himself for his piety was gone to dwell with the gods, and that his wife, and his daughter, and the helmsman partook of the same honour. And he commanded them that they should go to Babylon, and take up the scriptures which they had buried, and distribute them among men. Moreover, he told them that the land in which they stood was Armenia. And when they heard these things, they sacrificed to the gods and journeyed on foot to Babylon. But of the ship that grounded on the mountains of Armenia a part remains to this day, and some people scrape the bitumen off it and use it in charms. So when they were come to Babylon they dug up the scriptures in Sippar, and built many cities, and restored the sanctuaries, and repeopled Babylon."

According to the Greek historian Nicolaus of Damascus, a contemporary and friend of Augustus and of Herod the Great, "there is above Minyas in Armenia a great mountain called Baris, to which, as the story goes, many people fled for refuge in the Flood and were saved: they say, too, that a certain man, floating in an ark, grounded on the summit, and that remains of the timbers were preserved for a long time. The man may have been he who was recorded by Moses, the legislator of the Jews."[2] Whether Nicolaus of Damascus drew this information from Babylonian or Hebrew tradition may be doubted: the reference to Moses

---

[1] The Armenian text of Eusebius stretches the length of the ship to *fifteen* furlongs, or nearly two miles, which seems exorbitant when we consider the state of the shipbuilding industry in the days before the Flood. No modern dock would hold such a vessel.

[2] Nicolaus Damascenus, quoted by Josephus, *Antiquit. Jud.,* i, 3, 6; *Fragmenta Historicorum Graecorum,* ed. C. Müller, ii, 415, Frag. 76. For Minyas some scholars would substitute Milyas in the text, comparing Pliny, *Nat. Hist.,* v, 147, "*Attingit Galatia et Pamphyliae Cabaliam et Milyas qui circa Barim sunt.*" The reading Minyas is retained by C. Müller and defended by A. Reinach, *Noé Sangariou* (Paris, 1913), pp. 47 *sqq.*

seems to show that he was acquainted with the narrative in Genesis, which he may easily have learned through his patron Herod.

For many centuries the Babylonian tradition of a great flood was known to Western scholars only through its preservation in the Greek fragments of Berosus; it was reserved for modern times to recover the original Babylonian version from the long-lost archives of Assyria. In the course of those excavations at Nineveh, which were one of the glories of the nineteenth century, and which made an epoch in the study of ancient history, the English explorers were fortunate enough to discover extensive remains of the library of the great king Ashurbanipal, who reigned from 668 to 626 B.C. in the splendid sunset of the Assyrian empire, carrying the terror of his arms to the banks of the Nile, embellishing his capital with magnificent structures, and gathering within its walls from far and near a vast literature, historical, scientific, grammatical and religious, for the enlightenment of his people.[1] The literature, of which a great part was borrowed from Babylonian originals, was inscribed in cuneiform characters on tablets of soft clay, which were afterwards baked hard and deposited in the library. Apparently the library was arranged in an upper story of the palace, which, in the last sack of the city, collapsed in the flames, shattering the tablets to pieces in its fall. Many of them are still cracked and scorched by the heat of the burning ruins. In later ages the ruins were ransacked by antiquaries of the class of Dusterswivel, who sought among them for the buried treasures not of learning but of gold, and by their labours contributed still further to the disruption and disintegration of the precious records. To complete their destruction the rain, soaking through the ground every spring, saturates them with water containing chemicals, which form in every crack and fissure crystals that by their growth split the already broken tablets into minuter fragments. Yet by laboriously piecing together a multitude of these fragments George Smith, of the British Museum, was able to recompose the now famous epic of Gilgamesh in twelve cantos, or rather tablets, the eleventh of which contains the Babylonian story of the Deluge. The great discovery was announced by Mr. Smith at a meeting of the Society of Biblical Archaeology on December the 3rd, 1872.[2]

It was ingeniously conjectured by Sir Henry Rawlinson that the twelve cantos of the Gilgamesh epic corresponded to the twelve signs of the zodiac, so that the course of the poem followed, as it were, the course of the sun through the twelve months of the year. The theory is to some extent confirmed by the place assigned to the Flood legend in the eleventh canto; for the eleventh Babylonian month fell at the height of the rainy season, it was dedicated to the storm-god Ramman, and its name is said to signify " month of the curse of rain."[3] Be that

---

[1] Morris Jastrow, *The Religion of Babylonia and Assyria* (Boston, U.S.A., 1898), p. 43.

[2] George Smith, *The Chaldean Account of Genesis,* a new edition revised and corrected by A. H. Sayce (London, 1880), pp. 1 *sqq.*

[3] E. Schrader, *The Cuneiform Inscriptions and the Old Testament,* translated by O. C. Whitehouse (London and Edinburgh, 1885), i, 47 ; M. Jastrow, *The Religion of Babylonia and*

as it may, the story as it stands is an episode or digression destitute of all organic connection with the rest of the poem. It is introduced as follows.[1]

The hero of the poem, Gilgamesh, has lost his dear friend Engidu[2] by death, and he himself has fallen grievously sick. Saddened by the past and anxious for the future, he resolves to seek out his remote ancestor Ut-napishtim,[3] son of Ubara-Tutu, and to inquire of him how mortal man can attain to eternal life. For surely, he thought, Ut-napishtim must know the secret, since he has been made like to the gods and now dwells somewhere far away in blissful immortality. A weary and a perilous journey must Gilgamesh accomplish to come at him. He passes the mountain, guarded by a scorpion man and woman, where the sun goes down : he traverses a dark and dreadful road never trodden before by mortal man : he is ferried across a great sea : he crosses the Water of Death by a narrow bridge, and at last he enters the presence of Ut-napishtim.[4] But when he puts to his great ancestor the question, how man may attain to eternal life, he receives a discouraging reply : the sage tells him that immortality is not for man. Surprised at this answer from one who had been a man and was now himself immortal, Gilgamesh naturally asks his venerable relative to explain how he had contrived

Assyria (Boston, 1898), pp. 463, 484, 510 ; *id., Hebrew and Babylonian Myths*, p. 325, note [1]. According to Schrader, " the Akkadian name of the month, *iti aša šēgi*=Assyrian *aroh arrat zunni*, signifies 'month of the curse of rain,' *i.e.*, 'month of the judgment of the Flood.'" Further correspondences between the cantos and the months are noted by Professor Jastrow, *ll.cc.*

[1] For translations or summaries of the Deluge legend, see Eberhard Schrader, *The Cuneiform Inscriptions and the Old Testament*, translated by Rev. Owen C. Whitehouse (London and Edinburgh, 1885–1888), i, 46 *sqq.;* M. Jastrow, *The Religion of Babylonia and Assyria* (Boston, 1898), pp. 495 *sqq.; id., Hebrew and Babylonian Traditions* (London, 1914), pp. 325 *sqq.;* L. W. King, *Babylonian Religion and Mythology* (London, 1899), pp. 127 *sqq.;* P. Jensen, *Assyrisch-Babylonische Mythen und Epen* (Berlin, 1900), pp. 229 *sqq.;* W. Muss-Arnolt, in R. F. Harper's *Assyrian and Babylonian Literature* (New York, 1901), pp. 350 *sqq.;* H. Zimmern, in E. Schrader's *Die Keilinschriften und das Alte Testament*, Dritte Auflage (Berlin, 1902), pp. 544 *sqq.;* Alfred Jeremias, *Das Alte Testament im Lichte des Alten Orients*, Zweite Auflage (Berlin, 1906), pp. 228 *sqq.;* P. Dhorme, *Choix de Textes Religieux Assyro-Babyloniens* (Paris, 1907), pp. 100 *sqq.;* Arthur Ungnad, in H. Gressmann's *Altorientalische Texte und Bilder zum Alten Testamente* (Tübingen, 1909), i, 50 *sqq.;* A. Ungnad, *Das Gilgamesch-Epos* (Göttingen, 1911), pp. 52 *sqq.;* R. W. Rogers, *Cuneiform Parallels to the Old Testament* (Oxford [1912]), pp. 90 *sqq.* Of these works the translations of Jensen, Dhorme, and Rogers are accompanied by the original Babylonian text printed in Roman characters. The version in the text is based on a comparison of these various renderings.

[2] The name is said to be Sumerian, meaning " Enki (Semitic Ea) is Creator." See A. Ungnad und H. Gressmann, *Das Gilgamesch-Epos*, pp. 75 *sq.* The name was formerly read Eabani.

[3] The name is said to mean " He saw (*âta, ât*) life," in the sense of " He found life." See H. Zimmern, in E. Schrader's *Die Keilinschriften und das Alte Testament*,[3] p. 545, note [2]. Compare P. Jensen, *Assyrisch-Babylonische Mythen und Epen*, p. 466 ; A. Ungnad und H. Gressmann, *Das Gilgamesch-Epos*, p. 80. The name was formerly read as Par-napishtim, Per-napishtim, or Tsĭt-napishtim.

[4] As to the journey, narrated in the ninth and tenth cantos of the poem, see M. Jastrow *The Religion of Babylonia and Assyria*, pp. 487–492 ; L. W. King, *Babylonian Religion and Mythology*, pp. 165–171 ; A. Ungnad und H. Gressmann, *Das Gilamesch-Epos*, pp. 134–139.

to evade the common doom. It is in answer to this pointed question that Ut-napishtim tells the story of the Great Flood, which runs as follows :—

Ut-napishtim spoke to him, to Gilgamesh: "I will reveal to thee, O Gilgamesh, a hidden word, and the purpose[1] of the gods will I declare to thee. Shurippak, a city which thou knowest, which lies on the bank of the Euphrates, that city was old,[2] and the gods within it, their heart prompted the great gods to send a flood.[3] There was their father Anu, their counsellor the warrior Enlil,[4] their messenger Ninib, their prince Ennugi. The Lord of Wisdom, Ea, sat also with them, he repeated their word to the hut[5] of reeds, saying, 'O reed hut, reed hut, O wall, wall, O reed hut hearken, O wall attend. O man of Shurippak, son of Ubara-Tutu, pull down thy house, build a ship, forsake thy possessions, take heed for thy life! Thy gods abandon, save thy life, bring living seed of every kind into the ship. As for the ship which thou shalt build, well planned must be its dimensions, its breadth and its length shall bear proportions each to each, and thou shalt launch it in the ocean.'[6] I took heed and spake unto Ea, my lord, saying, 'The command, O my lord, which thou hast given, I will honour and will fulfil. But how shall I make answer unto the city, the people and the elders thereof?' Ea opened his mouth and spake, and he said unto me his servant, 'Thus shalt thou answer and say unto them: Because Enlil hates me, no longer may I abide in your city nor lay my head on Enlil's earth. Down into the deep sea must I go with Ea, my lord, to dwell.'" So Ut-napishtim obeyed the god Ea and gathered together the wood and all things needful for the building of the ship, and on the fifth day he laid down the hull. In the shape of a barge he built it, and on it he set a house a hundred and twenty cubits high, and he divided the house into six stories, and

---

[1] Or "decision" (M. Jastrow, R. W. Rogers), "secret" (P. Jensen, A. Jeremias, P. Dhorme, A. Ungnad), "mystery" (W. Muss-Arnolt). The same Assyrian word (*pirishtu*) occurs again twice towards the end of the canto. See below, p. 241. It may be connected with the Hebrew verb *parash* (פָּרַשׁ), "make distinct, declare," with which the lexicographers compare the Assyrian *parâsu*. See W. Gesenius, *Hebräisches und Aramäisches Handwörterbuch*,[14] ed., F. Buhl (Leipsic, 1905), p. 604. The "purpose" or "decision" in question is the resolve of the gods to bring a flood upon the world.

[2] H. Zimmern proposed, by a slight change of reading, to translate "that city was not pious" (E. Schrader, *Die Keilinschriften und das Alte Testament*,[3] p. 546, note [6]). This would assign the wickedness of the city as the cause of its destruction by the flood. But the suggested reading and rendering have not been accepted by later editors and translators.

[3] "Or the gods thereof induced the great gods to bring a cyclone over it" (M. Jastrow, *Hebrew and Babylonian Traditions*, p. 326).

[4] Or Illil, less correctly Ellil. The name was formerly read Bel (so Jensen and Dhorme, and formerly Jastrow). Enlil is the Sumerian name of the god, Bel is his Semitic name. Together with Anu, the Father of the Gods, and Enki (the Semitic Ea), he made up the highest trinity of the ancient Sumerians. See L. W. King, *Babylonian Religion and Mythology*, p. 14 ; A. Ungnad und H. Gressmann, *Das Gilgamesch-Epos*, p. 76.

[5] Or perhaps rather "fence." So Dhorme translates it, "*haie de roseaux.*" As to the hut or wall of reeds, see below, pp. 244 *sq.*

[6] Or "On a level with the deep, provide it with a covering" (M. Jastrow, *Hebrew and Babylonian Traditions*, p. 326). ". . . the ocean, cover it with a roof" (R. W. Rogers). Similarly A. Ungnad (*Das Gilgamesch-Epos*, p. 53).

in each story he made nine rooms. Water-plugs he fastened within it; the out-side he daubed with bitumen, and the inside he caulked with pitch. He caused oil to be brought, and he slaughtered oxen and lambs. He filled jars with sesame-wine and oil and grape-wine; he gave the people to drink like a river and he made a feast like to the feast of the New Year. And when the ship was ready he filled it with all he had of silver, and all that he had of gold, and all that he had of living seed. Also he brought up into the ship all his family and his household, the cattle of the field likewise and the beasts of the field, and the handicraftsmen: all of them he brought in. A fixed time the sun-god Shamash had appointed, saying, "'At eventide the lord of darkness will send a heavy rain. Then enter thou into the ship and shut thy door.' The time appointed drew near, and at eventide the lord of the darkness sent a heavy rain. Of the storm, I saw the beginning, to look upon the storm I was afraid. I entered into the ship and shut the door. To the pilot of the ship, even to Puzur-Amurri, the sailor, I committed the (floating) palace[1] and all that therein was. When the early dawn appeared there came up from the horizon a black cloud. Ramman[2] thundered in the midst thereof, the gods Mujati[3] and Lugal[4] went before. Like messengers they passed over mountain and land; Irragal[5] tore away the ship's post. There went Ninib and he made the storm to burst. The Anunnaki lifted up flaming torches, with the brightness thereof they lit up the earth The whirlwind of Ramman[2] mounted up into the heavens, and all light was turned into darkness." A whole day the tempest raged, and the waters rose on the mountains. "No man beheld his fellow, no more could men know each other. In heaven the gods were afraid of the deluge, they drew back, they climbed up into the heaven of Anu. The gods crouched like dogs, they cowered by the walls. Ishtar cried out like a woman in travail, loudly lamented the queen of the gods with her beautiful voice: Let that day be turned to clay, when[6] I commanded evil in the assembly of the gods! Alas, that I commanded evil in the assembly of the gods, that for the destruction of my

---

[1] The ship is so called because of its many stories and apartments. The Assyrian word here employed (*ekallu*) is the same with the ordinary Hebrew word for a palace or temple (הֵיכָל *hekal*). See E. Schrader, *The Cuneiform Inscriptions and the Old Testament,* i, 56; P. Dhorme, *Choix de Textes Religieux Assyro-Babyloniens,* p. 109, note [96]; Fr. Brown, S. R. Driver, and Ch. A. Briggs, *Hebrew and English Lexicon* (Oxford, 1906), p. 228.

[2] So L. W. King and A. Ungnad (*Das Gilgamesch-Epos,* p. 56). Others read "Adad" (so Jensen, Jeremias, and formerly Ungnad). Ramman or Adad was the god of thunder and storms. His name is written AN.IM. See A. Ungnad und H. Gressmann, *Das Gilgamesch-Epos,* p. 79.

[3] A minor deity, afterwards identified with Nabu (Nebo). See A. Ungnad und H. Gressmann, *Das Gilgamesch-Epos,* p. 78.

[4] A minor deity, the herald of the gods. His name means "King," a title bestowed on Marduk. Hence some translators render it by "Marduk" in the present passage. See A. Ungnad und H. Gressmann, *Das Gilgamesch-Epos,* p. 78.

[5] Irragal or Irrakal is "the Great Irra," the god of pestilence, more commonly known as Nergal. See A. Ungnad und H. Gressmann, *Das Gilgamesch-Epos,* pp. 77, 78.

[6] So Jensen, Dhorme, and Jastrow (*Hebrew and Babylonian Traditions,* p. 331). Others translate, "The former time (that is, the old race of man) has been turned into clay, because——"

people I commanded battle! That which I brought forth, where is it? Like the spawn of fish it filleth the sea. The gods of the Anunnaki[1] wept with her, the gods were bowed down, they sat down weeping. Their lips were pressed together. For six days and six nights the wind blew, and the deluge and the tempest overwhelmed the land. When the seventh day drew nigh, then ceased the tempest and the deluge and the storm, which had fought like a host. Then the sea grew quiet, it went down; the hurricane and the deluge ceased. I looked upon the sea, there was silence come,[2] and all mankind was turned back into clay. Instead of the fields a swamp lay before me.[3] I opened the window and the light fell upon my cheek; I bowed myself down, I sat down, I wept, over my cheek flowed my tears. I looked upon the world, and behold all was sea. After twelve (days?)[4] an island arose, to the land Nisir the ship made its way. The mount of Nisir[5] held the ship fast and let it not slip. The first day, the second day, the mountain Nisir held the ship fast: the third day, the fourth day, the mountain Nisir held the ship fast: the fifth day, the sixth day, the mountain Nisir held the ship fast. When the seventh day drew nigh, I sent out a dove, and let her go forth. The dove flew hither and thither, but there was no resting-place for her and she returned. Then I sent out a swallow and let her go forth. The swallow flew hither and thither, but there was no resting-place for her, and she returned. Then I sent out a raven and let her go forth. The raven flew away, she beheld the abatement of the waters, she ate,[6] she waded, she croaked, but she did not return. Then I brought all out unto the four winds, I offered an offering, I made a libation on the peak of the mountain. By sevens I set out the vessels, under them I heaped up reed, and cedar-wood, and myrtle.[7] The gods smelt the savour, the gods smelt the sweet savour. The gods gathered like flies about him that offered up the sacrifice. Then the Lady of the gods drew nigh, she lifted up the great jewels which Anu had made according to her wish. She said, 'Oh ye gods here, as truly as I will not forget the jewels of *lapis lazuli* which are on my neck, so truly will I remember these days, never shall I forget them! Let the gods come

---

[1] Or "because of the Anunnaki" (P. Dhorme), "over the Anunnaki" (W. Muss-Arnolt).

[2] Or "and cried aloud" (so L. W. King, W. Muss-Arnolt, and doubtfully A. Jeremias).

[3] "The swamp reached to the roofs" (so P. Dhorme), "Like a roof the plain lay level" (R. W. Rogers). See E. Schrader, *The Cuneiform Inscriptions and the Old Testament*, translated by O. C. Whitehouse (London and Edinburgh, 1885), i, 54.

[4] "Double hours" (so P. Jensen and H. Zimmern). Dhorme thinks that the number refers to distance: the island appeared twelve miles or leagues(?) away. This interpretation is now accepted by M. Jastrow (*Hebrew and Babylonian Traditions*, p. 332).

[5] If Haupt and Delitsch are right, the name Nisir is derived from the same root as the Hebrew *nasar* (נָצַר), meaning "to guard, keep, preserve"; so that Mount Nisir would be "the Mount of Salvation or Deliverance." Similarly in Greek legend, Deucalion is said to have dedicated an altar to Zeus the Deliverer on the mountain where he landed after the great flood. See below, p. 264.

[6] So P. Jensen, H. Zimmern, P. Dhorme, and A. Ungnad. "She drew near" (R. W. Rogers). "She came near" (L. W. King).

[7] Or "incense" (so L. W. King).

to the offering, but Enlil[1] shall not come to the offering, for he took not counsel and sent the deluge, and my people he gave to destruction.' Now when Enlil[1] drew nigh, he saw the ship; then was Enlil[1] wroth. He was filled with anger against the gods, the Igigi (saying), 'Who then hath escaped with his life? No man shall live after the destruction.' Then Ninib opened his mouth and spake, he said to the warrior Enlil,[1] 'Who but Ea could have done this thing? For Ea knoweth every matter.' Then Ea opened his mouth and spake, he said to the warrior Enlil,[1] 'Thou art the governor of the gods,[2] O warrior, but thou wouldst not take counsel and thou hast sent the deluge! On the sinner visit his sin, and on the transgressor visit his transgression. But hold thy hand that all be not destroyed! and forbear, that all be not confounded! Instead of sending a deluge let a lion come and minish mankind! Instead of sending a deluge, let a leopard[3] come and minish mankind! Instead of sending a deluge, let a famine come and waste the land! Instead of sending a deluge, let the Plague-god come and slay mankind! I did not reveal the purpose[4] of the great gods. I caused Atrakhasis[5] to see a dream, and thus he heard the purpose[4] of the gods.' Thereupon Enlil[6] arrived at a decision, and he went up into the ship. He took my hand and brought me forth, he brought my wife forth, he made her to kneel at my side, he turned towards us,[7]

---

[1] Or "Bel." So M. Jastrow, L. W. King, P. Jensen, and P. Dhorme. See above, p. 238, note [4].

[2] Or "Thou wise one among the gods" (so W. Muss-Arnolt, H. Zimmern, A. Jeremias, P. Dhorme, A. Ungnad, R. W. Rogers). This rendering certainly gives more point, as P. Dhorme observes, to what follows: "You so wise, yet to be so rash and unjust as to send the deluge!" The doubtful Assyrian word is *abkallu*, which, according to Delitsch, means "commander," "ruler," but according to others has the sense of "wise." See P. Jensen, *Assyrisch-Babylonische Mythen und Epen*, p. 320; P. Dhorme, *Choix de Textes religieux Assyro-Babyloniens*, p. 117.

[3] The meaning of the Assyrian word (*barbaru*), here translated "leopard," is uncertain. Ungnad and Rogers render "wolf"; Jeremias prefers a panther, Jastrow a jackal, and Muss-Arnolt a tiger. The rendering "leopard" is strongly defended by P. Dhorme.

[4] Or "secret." See above, p. 238, footnote [1].

[5] "The very prudent one," a name or title applied to Ut-napishtim. See below, p. 242, note [1].

[6] Or "Bel." So M. Jastrow, L. W. King, P. Jensen, W. Muss-Arnolt, H. Zimmern, A. Jeremias, and P. Dhorme. Ungnad and Rogers read "Ea" instead of Enlil (Bel). But the sense given by the former reading is incomparably finer. Enlil (Bel) is at first enraged at the escape of Ut-napishtim and his family, but, moved by Ea's eloquent pleading on their behalf, he experiences a revulsion of feeling, and entering the ship he magnanimously takes Ut-napishtim by the hand and leads him forth. The dramatic situation thus created is worthy of a great literary artist, and reminds us of the famous meeting of Achilles and Priam in Homer, "His hand he placed in the old man's hand, and pushed him gently away" (*Iliad*, xxiv, 508). The phrase rendered "arrived at a decision" (so L. W. King, W. Muss-Arnolt, and apparently H. Zimmern) is variously translated "came to his senses" (so A. Jeremias and formerly M. Jastrow), "then they took his counsel" (P. Jensen and P. Dhorme), and "now take counsel for him" (so A. Ungnad, R. W. Rogers, and now M. Jastrow, in *Hebrew and Babylonian Traditions*, p. 334). This last rendering ("Now take counsel for him") puts the words in the mouth of the preceding speaker Ea: so understood, they are at once feeble and otiose, whereas understood to refer to the sudden revulsion of feeling in Enlil (Bel), they are eminently in place, and add a powerful stroke to the picture.

[7] Or "turned us face to face" (W. Muss-Arnolt), "turned us toward each other" (R. W.

he stood between us, he blessed us (saying), 'Hitherto hath Ut-napishtim been a man, but now let Ut-napishtim and his wife be like unto the gods, even us, and let Ut-napishtim dwell afar off at the mouth of the rivers!' Then they took me, and afar off, at the mouth of the rivers, they made me to dwell."

Such is the long story of the Deluge interwoven into the Gilgamesh epic, with which, to all appearance, it had originally no connexion. A fragment of another version of the tale is preserved on a broken tablet, which, like the tablets of the Gilgamesh epic, was found among the ruins of Ashurbanipal's library at Nineveh. It contains a part of the conversation which is supposed to have taken place before the flood between the god Ea and the Babylonian Noah, who is here called Atrakhasis, a name which, as we saw, is incidentally applied to him in the Gilgamesh epic, though elsewhere in that version he is named not Atrakhasis but Ut-napishtim. The name Atrakhasis is said to be the Babylonian original which in Berosus's Greek version of the Deluge legend is represented by Xisuthrus.[1] In this fragment the god Ea commands Atrakhasis, saying, "Go in and shut the door of the ship. Bring within thy corn, thy goods and thy possessions, thy (wife?), thy family, thy kinsfolk, and thy craftsmen. the cattle of the field, the beasts of the field, as many as eat grass."[2] In his reply the hero says that he has never built a ship before, and he begs that a plan of the ship be drawn for him on the ground, which he may follow in laying down the vessel.[3]

Thus far the Babylonian versions of the flood legend date only from the time of Ashurbanipal in the seventh century before our era, and might therefore conceivably be of later origin than the Hebrew version and copied from it. However, conclusive evidence of the vastly greater antiquity of the Babylonian legend is furnished by a broken tablet, which was discovered at Abu-Habbah, the site of the ancient city of Sippar, in the course of excavations undertaken by the Turkish Government. The tablet contains a very mutilated version of the flood story,

Rogers), "touched our face" (P. Dhorme), "touched our foreheads" (A. Ungnad, M. Jastrow, in *Hebrew and Babylonian Traditions*, p. 334), "touched our *shoulder*" (P. Jensen).

[1] Atrakhasis, "the very prudent one," in the inverted form Khasis-atra is identified with Xisuthrus by E. Schrader, H. Zimmern, P. Dhorme, and A. Ungnad. See E. Schrader, *The Cuneiform Inscriptions and the Old Testament*, i, 56 ; H. Zimmern, in E. Schrader's *Die Keilinschriften und das Alte Testament*, Dritte Auflage, pp. 532, 551 ; P. Dhorme, *Choix de Textes religieux Assyro-Babyloniens*, pp. 119 note [196], 132 note [53] ; A. Ungnad, in H. Gressmann's *Altorientalische Texte und Bilder zum Alten Testamente*, i, 39 note [15], 46 note [4] ; A. Ungnad und H. Gressmann, *Das Gilgamesch-Epos*, pp. 59, 74 *sq.* As to the name Atrakhasis, see further P. Jensen, *Assyrisch-Babylonische Mythen und Epen*, pp. 276 *sq. ;* H. Usener, *Die Sintflutsagen*, p. 15.

[2] "As many as eat grass." So P. Jensen, A. Jeremias, A. Ungnad, and R. W. Rogers. Others render simply, "all kinds of herbs," understanding the words as a direction to Atrakhasis to take on board a supply of vegetables. So P. Dhorme and M. Jastrow.

[3] P. Jensen, *Assyrisch-Babylonische Mythen und Epen*, pp. 255, 257 ; A. Jeremias, *Das Alte Testament im Lichte des Alten Orients*,[2] p. 233 ; P. Dhorme, *Choix de Textes religieux Assyro-Babyloniens*, pp. 126 *sq. ;* A. Ungnad, in H. Gressmann's *Altorientalische Texte und Bilder zum Alten Testamente*, i, 57 ; A. Ungnad und H. Gressmann, *Das Gilgamesch-Epos*, p. 69 ; R. W. Rogers, *Cuneiform Parallels to the Old Testament*, pp. 103 *sq.* ; M. Jastrow, *Hebrew and Babylonian Traditions*, pp. 343–345.

and it is exactly dated; for at the end there is a colophon or note recording that the tablet was written on the twenty-eighth day of the month Shabatu (the eleventh Babylonian month) in the eleventh year of King Ammizaduga, or about 1966 B.C. Unfortunately the text is so fragmentary that little information can be extracted from it; but the name of Atrakhasis occurs in it, together with references to the great rain and apparently to the ship and the entrance into it of the people who were to be saved.[1]

Yet another very ancient version of the deluge legend came to light at Nippur in the excavations conducted by the University of Pennsylvania. It is written on a small fragment of unbaked clay, and on the ground of the style of writing and of the place where the tablet was found it is dated by its discoverer, Professor H. V. Hilprecht, not later than 2100 B.C. In this fragment a god appears to announce that he will cause a deluge which will sweep away all mankind at once; and he warns the person whom he addresses to build a great ship, with a strong roof, in which he is to save his life, and also to bring the beasts of the field and the birds of heaven.[2]

All these versions of the flood story are written in the Semitic language of Babylonia and Assyria; but another fragmentary version, found by the American excavators at Nippur and recently deciphered, is written in Sumerian, that is, in the non-Semitic language of the ancient people who appear to have preceded the Semites in Babylonia and to have founded in the lower valley of the Euphrates that remarkable system of civilization which we commonly call Babylonian.[3] The city

---

[1] L. W. King, *Babylonian Religion and Mythology*, pp. 124–126; P. Jensen, *Assyrisch-Babylonische Mythen und Epen*, pp. 289, 291; H. Zimmern, in E. Schrader's *Die Keilinschriften und das Alte Testament*,³ p. 552; P. Dhorme, *Choix de Textes religieux Assyro-Babyloniens*, pp. 120–125; A. Ungnad, in H. Gressmann's *Altorientalische Texte und Bilder zum Alten Testamente*, i, 57 *sq.*; A. Ungnad und H. Gressmann, *Das Gilgamesch-Epos*, pp. 5 *sq.*, 69 *sq.*; R. W. Rogers, *Cuneiform Parallels to the Old Testament*, pp. 104–107; M. Jastrow, *Hebrew and Babylonian Traditions*, pp. 340 *sq.* The date of King Ammizaduga, the tenth monarch of the first Babylonian dynasty, is variously given as 2100 B.C. (so H. Zimmern) or somewhat later than 2000 B.C. (so A. Ungnad, *Das Gilgamesch-Epos*, p. 5). Professor Ed. Meyer assigns the king's reign to the years 1812–1792 B.C. (*Geschichte des Altertums*,² i, 2, p. 574); and accordingly R. W. Rogers and M. Jastrow date the king roughly at 1800 B.C. According to the latest calculation, based on elaborate astronomical data, the year of Ammizaduga's accession is now assigned by Mr. L. W. King to the year 1977 B.C., and in this dating ordinary students may provisionally acquiesce. See L. W. King, *A History of Babylon* (London, 1915), pp. 107 *sqq.*

[2] A. Ungnad und H. Gressmann, *Das Gilgamesch-Epos*, pp. 6, 73; R. W. Rogers, *Cuneiform Parallels to the Old Testament*, pp. 108 *sq.*; M. Jastrow, *Hebrew and Babylonian Traditions*, pp. 342 *sq.* These scholars incline to date the tablet later than 2100 B.C. "The tablet may well be as old as Professor Hilprecht argues, but the suggestion of a date so late as the early Kassite period (1700 B.C.) can hardly be excluded" (R. W. Rogers, *op. cit.*, p. 108).

[3] The tablet containing the Sumerian version of the story was first read by Dr. Arno Poebel, of the Johns Hopkins University, in 1912. See A. Poebel, "The Babylonian Story of the Creation and the Earliest History of the World," *The Museum Journal*, Philadelphia, June, 1913, pp. 41 *sqq.*; *id.*, in *University of Pennsylvania, Publications of the Babylonian Section of the University Museum*, vol. iv, No. 1 (Philadelphia, 1914), pp. 7–70; M. Jastrow, *Hebrew and Babylonian Traditions*, pp. 335 *sqq.*; L. W. King, "Recent Babylonian Research and its Relation to Hebrew Studies," *Church Quarterly Review*, No. 162, January, 1916, pp. 271 *sqq.*

of Nippur, where the Sumerian version of the deluge legend has been discovered, was the holiest and perhaps the oldest religious centre in the country, and the city-god Enlil was the head of the Babylonian pantheon.   The tablet which records the legend would seem, from the character of the script, to have been written about the time of the famous Hammurabi, king of Babylon, that is, about 2100 B.C.   But the story itself must be very much older; for by the close of the third millennium before our era, when the tablet was inscribed, the Sumerians as a separate race had almost ceased to exist, having been absorbed in the Semitic population, and their old tongue was already a dead language, though the ancient literature and sacred texts embalmed in it were still studied and copied by the Semitic priests and scribes.[1] Hence the discovery of a Sumerian version of the deluge legend raises a presumption that the legend itself dates from a time anterior to the occupation of the Euphrates valley by the Semites, who after their immigration into the country appear to have borrowed the story from their predecessors the Sumerians.   It is of interest to observe that the Sumerian version of the flood story formed a sequel to an account, unfortunately very fragmentary, of the creation of man, according to which men were created by the gods before the animals.   Thus the Sumerian story agrees with the Hebrew account in Genesis, in so far as both of them treat the creation of man and the great flood as events closely connected with each other in the early history of the world; and further, the Sumerian narrative agrees with the Jehovistic against the Priestly Document in representing the creation of man as antecedent to the creation of the animals.[2]

Only the lower half of the tablet on which this Sumerian Genesis was inscribed has as yet come to light, but enough remains to furnish us with the main outlines of the flood story.   From it we learn that Ziugiddu, or rather Ziudsuddu,[3] was at once a king and a priest of the god Enki, the Sumerian deity who was the equivalent of the Semitic Ea,[4] daily he occupied himself in the god's service, prostrating himself in humility and constant in his observance at the shrine.   To reward him for his piety Enki informs him that at the request of Enlil it has been resolved in the council of the gods to destroy the seed of mankind by a rain-storm. Before the holy man receives this timely warning his divine friend bids him take his stand beside a wall, saying, "Stand by the wall on my left side, and at the wall I will speak a word with thee."   These words are evidently connected with the

---

[1] L. W. King, "Recent Babylonian Research and its Relation to Hebrew Studies," *Church Quarterly Review*, No. 162, January, 1916, pp. 274, 275.   As to the date of Hammurabi (about 2100 B.C.) see Principal J. Skinner, *Commentary on Genesis* (Edinburgh, 1910), p. xiv, note † ; S. R. Driver, *The Book of Genesis*[10] (London, 1916), p. 156 ; R. Kittel, *Geschichte des Volkes Israel*,[2] i (Gotha, 1912), p. 77 ; L. W. King, *A History of Babylon* (London, 1915), pp. 111, 320, who assigns the king's reign to 2123–2081 B.C.   A later date (1958–1916 B.C.) is assigned to Hammurabi's reign by Professor Ed. Meyer (*Geschichte des Altertums*,[2] i, 2, p. 557).

[2] Genesis ii (Jehovistic) compared with Genesis i (Priestly Document).

[3] So Mr. L. W. King would read the name (*Church Quarterly Review*, No. 162, January, 1916, p. 277).

[4] L. W. King, *Babylonian Religion and Mythology*, p. 14.   See above, p. 238, note [4].

curious passage in the Semitic version, where Ea begins his warning to Ut-napishtim, " O reed hut, reed hut, O wall, wall, O reed hut hearken, O wall attend."[1] Together the parallel passages suggest that the friendly god, who might not directly betray the resolution of the gods to a mortal man, adopted the subterfuge of whispering it to a wall of reeds, on the other side of which he had first stationed Ziudsuddu. Thus by eavesdropping the good man learned the fatal secret, while his divine patron was able afterwards to protest that he had not revealed the counsel of the gods. The subterfuge reminds us of the well-known story, how the servant of King Midas detected the ass's ears of his master, and, unable to contain himself, whispered the secret into a hole in the ground and filled up the hole with earth; but a bed of reeds grew up on the spot, and rustling in the wind, proclaimed to all the world the king's deformity.[2] The part of the tablet which probably described the building of the ship and Ziudsuddu's embarkation is lost, and in the remaining portion we are plunged into the midst of the Deluge. The storms of wind and rain are described as raging together. Then the text continues : " When for seven days, for seven nights, the rain-storm had raged in the land, when the great boat had been carried away by the wind-storms on the mighty waters, the Sun-god came forth, shedding light over heaven and earth." When the light shines into the boat, Ziudsuddu prostrates himself before the Sun-god and sacrifices an ox and a sheep. Then follows a gap in the text, after which we read of Ziudsuddu, the King, prostrating himself before the gods Anu and Enlil. The anger of Enlil against men appears now to be abated, for, speaking of Ziudsuddu, he says, " Life like that of a god I give to him," and " an eternal soul like that of a god I create for him," which means that the hero of the deluge legend, the Sumerian Noah, receives the boon of immortality, if not of divinity. Further, he is given the title of " Preserver of the Seed of Mankind," and the gods cause him to dwell on a mountain, perhaps the mountain of Dilmun, though the reading of the name is uncertain. The end of the legend is wanting.

Thus in its principal features the Sumerian version of the deluge legend agrees with the much longer and more circumstantial version preserved in the Gilgamesh epic. In both a great god (Enlil or Bel) resolves to destroy mankind by flooding the earth with rain ; in both another god (Enki or Ea) warns a man of the coming catastrophe, and the man, accepting the admonition, is saved in a ship ; in both the flood lasts at its height for seven days ; in both, when the deluge has abated, the man offers sacrifices and is finally raised to the rank of the gods. The only essential difference is in the name of the hero, who in the Sumerian version is called Ziudsuddu, and in the Semitic version Ut-napishtim or Atrakhasis. The

[1] Above, p. 238. With reference to the collocation of reeds and wall, it is well to remember that in ancient Babylonian buildings reed mats were regularly interposed between the layers of brick, at intervals of four or five feet, in order to protect the earthen mass from disintegration. So well known is this to the modern Arabs, that they give the name of *Buwariyya* or " reed mats " to ancient mounds in which this mode of construction is discernible. See W. K. Loftus, *Travels and Researches in Chaldaea and Susiana* (London, 1857), p. 168.

[2] Ovid, *Metamorphoses*, xi, 174 *sqq.*

Sumerian name Ziudsuddu resembles the name Xisuthrus, which Berosus gives as that of the hero who was saved from the flood; if the two names are really connected, we have fresh ground for admiring the fidelity with which the Babylonian historian followed the most ancient documentary sources.

The discovery of this very interesting tablet, with its combined accounts of the Creation and the Deluge, renders it highly probable that the narratives of the early history of the world which we find in Genesis did not originate with the Semites, but were borrowed by them from the older civilized people whom, some thousands of years before our era, the wild Semitic hordes, swarming out of the Arabian desert, found in possession of the fat lands of the lower Euphrates valley, and from whom the descendants of these primitive Bedouins gradually learned the arts and habits of civilization, just as the northern barbarians acquired a varnish of culture through their settlement in the Roman empire.

The various fragmentary versions, Babylonian and Sumerian, of the deluge story confirm the conclusion that the legend circulated independently of the Gilgamesh epic, into which the poet loosely inserted it as an episode. In the epic the original scene of the disaster is laid, as we saw, at the city of Shurippak on the Euphrates. Recent excavations of the German Oriental Society have revealed the site of the ancient city. The place is at the hill of Fara, to the north of Uruk, and the remains which have come to light there seem to show that Shurippak was among the very oldest Sumerian settlements yet discovered; for the inscribed clay tablets which have been excavated on the spot are of a very archaic character, and are believed to have been written not much later than 3400 B.C.[1] The site is now a long way from the sea and at some distance from the Euphrates; but we know that in the course of ages the river has repeatedly changed its bed, and that the sea has retreated, or rather that the land has advanced, in consequence of the vast quantities of soil annually washed down by the Euphrates and the Tigris.[2] Apparently the ancient city perished, not by water, but by fire; for the ruins are buried under a thick layer of ashes. After the conflagration the greater part of the hill seems to have remained desolate, though a small town existed on the spot during the Sumerian and Accadian periods. From about the time of Hammurabi, that is, from about 2100 B.C. onward, the very name of Shurippak vanishes from Babylonian history.[3] Thus the story of the great flood which destroyed the city cannot have originated later than the end of the third millennium before Christ, and it may well have been very much older. In the Sumerian version of the deluge legend Shurippak is named, along with Eridu, Larak, and Sippar, as cities before the flood; but in the fragmentary state of the

---

[1] A. Ungnad und H. Gressmann, *Das Gilgamesch-Epos*, pp. 190 *sq.*

[2] T. H. Huxley, "Hasisadra's Adventure," *Collected Essays*, vol, iv (London, 1911), pp. 250 *sq.*: Eduard Suess, *The Face of the Earth*, i (Oxford, 1904), pp. 24 *sq.*; G. Maspero, *Histoire Ancienne des peuples de l'Orient Classique, Les Origines* (Paris, 1895), pp. 552 *sq.*; Ed. Meyer, *Geschichte des Altertums*,[2] i, 2 (Stuttgart und Berlin, 1909), pp. 398 *sq.*

[3] A. Ungnad und H. Gressmann, *Das Gilgamesch-Epos*, p. 191.

text it is impossible to say whether or not it was the city of Ziudsuddu, the Sumerian Noah.[1]

§3. THE HEBREW STORY OF A GREAT FLOOD.

The ancient Hebrew legend of a great flood, as it is recorded in the book of Genesis,[2] runs thus:—

" *And the Lord saw that the wickedness of man was great in the earth, and that every imagination of the thoughts of his heart was only evil continually. And it repented the Lord that he had made man on the earth, and it grieved him at his heart. And the Lord said, I will destroy man whom I have created from the face of the ground; both man and beast, and creeping thing, and fowl of the air; for it repenteth me that I have made them. But Noah found grace in the eyes of the Lord.*

" These are the generations of Noah. Noah was a righteous man and perfect in his generations. Noah walked with God. And Noah begat three sons, Shem, Ham, and Japheth. And the earth was corrupt before God, and the earth was filled with violence. And God saw the earth, and behold, it was corrupt; for all flesh had corrupted his way upon the earth. And God said unto Noah, The end of all flesh is come before me; for the earth is filled with violence through them; and, behold, I will destroy them with the earth. Make thee an ark of gopher wood; rooms shalt thou make in the ark, and shalt pitch it within and without with pitch. And this is how thou shalt make it: the length of the ark three hundred cubits, the breadth of it fifty cubits, and the height of it thirty cubits. A light shalt thou make to the ark, and to a cubit shalt thou finish it upward; and the door of the ark shalt thou set in the side thereof; with lower, second, and third stories shalt thou make it. And I, behold, I do bring the flood of waters upon the earth, to destroy all flesh, wherein is the breath of life, from under heaven, every thing that is in the earth shall die. But I will establish my covenant with thee; and thou shalt come into the ark, thou, and thy sons, and thy wife, and thy sons' wives with thee. And of every living thing of all flesh, two of every sort shalt thou bring into the ark, to keep them alive with thee; they shall be male and female. Of the fowl after their kind, and of the cattle after their kind, of every creeping thing of the ground after its kind, two of every sort shall come unto thee, to keep them alive. And take thou unto thee of all food that is eaten, and gather it to thee; and it shall be for food for thee, and for them. Thus did Noah; according to all that God commanded him, so did he.

" *And the Lord said unto Noah, Come thou and all thy house into the ark; for thee have I seen righteous before me in this generation. Of every clean beast thou shalt take to thee seven and seven, the male and his female; and of the beasts that are not clean two, the male and his female; of the fowl also of the air, seven and seven,* male

---

[1] A. Poebel, in *The University of Pennsylvania, Publications of the Babylonian Section of the University Museum*, vol. iv, No. 1 (Philadelphia, 1914), pp. 18, 44.

[2] Genesis vi, 5–ix, 17, Revised Version.

and female : *to keep seed alive upon the face of all the earth. For yet seven days, and I will cause it to rain upon the earth forty days and forty nights ; and every living thing that I have made will I destroy from off the face of the ground. And Noah did according unto all that the Lord commanded him.* And Noah was six hundred years old when the flood of waters was upon the earth. *And Noah went in, and his sons, and his wife, and his sons' wives with him, into the ark, because of the waters of the flood. Of clean beasts, and of beasts that are not clean, and of fowls, and of every thing that creepeth upon the ground, there went in* two and two *unto Noah into the ark,* male and female, *as* God *commanded Noah. And it came to pass after the seven days, that the waters of the flood were upon the earth.* In the six hundredth year of Noah's life, in the second month, on the seventeenth day of the month, on the same day were all the fountains of the great deep broken up, and the windows of heaven were opened. *And the rain was upon the earth forty days and forty nights.*

" In the selfsame day entered Noah, and Shem, and Ham, and Japheth, the sons of Noah, and Noah's wife, and the three wives of his sons with them, into the ark ; they, and every beast after its kind, and all the cattle after their kind, and every creeping thing that creepeth upon the earth after its kind, and every fowl after its kind, every bird of every sort. And they went in unto Noah into the ark, two and two of all flesh, wherein is the breath of life. And they that went in, went in male and female of all flesh, as God commanded him : *and the Lord shut him in.* And the flood was forty days upon the earth ; *and the waters increased, and bare up the ark, and it was lift up above the earth.* And the waters prevailed, and increased greatly upon the earth ; and the ark went upon the face of the waters. And the waters prevailed exceedingly upon the earth ; and all the high mountains that were under the whole heaven were covered. Fifteen cubits upward did the waters prevail ; and the mountains were covered. And all flesh died that moved upon the earth, both fowl, and cattle, and beast, and every creeping thing that creepeth upon the earth, and every man : *all in whose nostrils was the breath of the spirit of life, of all that was in the dry land, died. And every living thing was destroyed which was upon the face of the ground, both man, and cattle, and creeping thing, and fowl of the heaven ; and they were destroyed from the earth : and Noah only was left, and they that were with him in the ark.* And the waters prevailed upon the earth an hundred and fifty days.

" And God remembered Noah, and every living thing, and all the cattle that were with him in the ark : and God made a wind to pass over the earth, and the waters assuaged ; the fountains also of the deep and the windows of heaven were stopped, *and the rain from heaven was restrained ; and the waters returned from off the earth continually :* and after the end of an hundred and fifty days the waters decreased. And the ark rested in the seventh month, on the seventeenth day of the month, upon the mountains of Ararat. And the waters decreased continually until the tenth month : in the tenth month, on the first day of the month, were the tops of the mountains seen. *And it came to pass at the end of forty days, that*

Noah opened the window of the ark which he had made: and he sent forth a raven, and it went forth to and fro, until the waters were dried up from off the earth. And he sent forth a dove from him, to see if the waters were abated from off the face of the ground; but the dove found no rest for the sole of her foot, and she returned unto him to the ark, for the waters were on the face of the whole earth: and he put forth his hand, and took her, and brought her in unto him into the ark. And he stayed yet other seven days; and again he sent forth the dove out of the ark; and the dove came into him at eventide; and, lo, in her mouth an olive leaf pluckt off: so Noah knew that the waters were abated from off the earth. And he stayed yet other seven days; and sent forth the dove; and she returned not again unto him any more. And it came to pass in the six hundred and first year, in the first month, the first day of the month, the waters were dried up from off the earth: *and Noah removed the covering of the ark, and looked, and, behold, the face of the ground was dried.* And in the second month, on the seven and twentieth day of the month, was the earth dry.

"And God spake unto Noah, saying, Go forth of the ark, thou, and thy wife, and thy sons, and thy sons' wives with thee. Bring forth with thee every living thing that is with thee of all flesh, both fowl, and cattle, and every creeping thing that creepeth upon the earth; that they may breed abundantly in the earth, and be fruitful, and multiply upon the earth. And Noah went forth, and his sons, and his wife, and his sons' wives with him: every beast, every creeping thing, and every fowl, whatsoever moveth upon the earth, after their families, went forth out of the ark. *And Noah builded an altar unto the Lord; and took of every clean beast, and of every clean fowl, and offered burnt offerings on the altar. And the Lord smelled the sweet savour; and the Lord said in his heart, I will not again curse the ground any more for man's sake, for that the imagination of man's heart is evil from his youth; neither will I again smite any more every thing living, as I have done. While the earth remaineth, seedtime and harvest, and cold and heat, and summer and winter, and day and night shall not cease.*

"And God blessed Noah and his sons, and said unto them, Be fruitful, and multiply, and replenish the earth. And the fear of you and the dread of you shall be upon every beast of the earth, and upon every fowl of the air; with all where-with the ground teemeth, and all the fishes of the sea, into your hand are they delivered. Every moving thing that liveth shall be food for you; as the green herb have I given you all. But flesh with the life thereof, which is the blood thereof, shall ye not eat. And surely your blood, the blood of your lives, will I require; at the hand of every beast will I require it: and at the hand of man, even at the hand of every man's brother, will I require the life of man. Whoso sheddeth man's blood, by man shall his blood be shed: for in the image of God made he man. And you, be ye fruitful, and multiply; bring forth abundantly in the earth, and multiply therein.

"And God spake unto Noah, and to his sons with him, saying, And I, behold, I establish my covenant with you, and with your seed after you; and with every living creature that is with you, the fowl, the cattle, and every beast of the earth with you; of all that go out of the ark, even every beast of the earth. And I will establish my covenant with you; neither shall all flesh be cut off any more by the waters of the flood; neither shall there any more be a flood to destroy the earth. And God said, This is the token of the covenant which I make between me and you and every living creature that is with you, for perpetual generations : I do set my bow in the cloud, and it shall bie for a token of a covenant between me and the earth. And it shall come to pass, when I bring a cloud over the earth, that the bow shall be seen in the cloud, and I will remember my covenant, which is between me and you and every living creature of all flesh; and the waters shall no more become a flood to destroy all flesh. And the bow shall be in the cloud; and I will look upon it, that I may remember the everlasting covenant between God and every living creature of all flesh that is upon the earth. And God said unto Noah, This is the token of the covenant which I have established between me and all flesh that is on the earth."

In this account of the Deluge Biblical critics are now agreed in detecting the presence of two originally distinct and to some extent inconsistent narratives, which have been combined so as to present the superficial appearance of a single homogeneous story. Yet the editorial task of uniting them has been performed so clumsily that the repetitions and inconsistencies left standing in them can hardly fail to attract the attention even of a careless reader. In reproducing the text of the legend from the English Revised Version I have distinguished the two strands of the composite narrative by printing them in different types; the analysis thus exhibited is the one now generally accepted by critics.[1]

Of the two versions of the legend thus artificially combined, the one, printed in ordinary Roman type, is derived from what the critics call the Priestly Code (usually designated by the letter P); the other, printed in italic type, is derived from what the critics call the Jehovistic or Jahwistic document (usually designated by the letter J), which is characterized by the use of the divine name Jehovah (Jahweh, or, rather, Yahweh). The two documents differ conspicuously in character and style, and they belong to different ages; for while the Jehovistic narrative is probably the oldest, the Priestly Code is now generally admitted to be the latest, of the four principal documents which have been united to form the Hexateuch. The Jehovistic document is believed to have been written in Judea in the early

---

[1] W. Robertson Smith, *The Old Testament in the Jewish Church*[2] (London and Edinburgh, 1892), pp. 329 *sq.*; E. Kautsch und A. Socin, *Die Genesis, mit äusserer Unterscheidung der Quellenschriften*[2] (Freiburg i. B., 1891), pp. 11 *sqq.*; E. Kautsch, *Die heilige Schrift des Alten Testaments übersetzt und herausgegeben* (Freiburg i. B. und Leipzig, 1894), pp. 6 *sqq.*; J. Estlin Carpenter and G. Harford-Battersby, *The Hexateuch* (London, 1900), ii, 9 *sqq.*; W. H. Bennett, *Genesis*, pp. 135 *sqq.* (*The Century Bible*); W. H. Bennett and W. F. Adeney, *A Biblical Introduction*[5] (London, 1908), pp. 27 *sqq.*; S. R. Driver, *The Book of Genesis*[10] (London, 1916), pp. 85 *sqq.*; id., *Introduction to the Literature of the Old Testament*[9] (Edinburgh, 1913), p. 14 ; K. Budde, *Geschichte des althebräischen Litteratur* (Leipzig, 1906), pp. 47 *sqq.*; J. Skinner, *Critical and Exegetical Commentary on Genesis* (Edinburgh, 1910), pp. 147 *sqq.*; M. Jastrow, *Hebrew and Babylonian Traditions* (London, 1914), pp. 348 *sqq.*

times of the Hebrew monarchy, probably in the ninth or eighth century before our era; the Priestly Code dates from the period after the year 586 B.C., when Jerusalem was taken by Nebuchadnezzar, King of Babylon, and the Jews were carried away by him into captivity. Both documents are in their form historical, but while the Jehovistic writer displays a genuine interest in the characters and adventures of the men and women whom he describes, the Priestly writer appears to concern himself with them only so far as he deemed them instruments in the great scheme of Providence for conveying to Israel a knowledge of God and of the religious and social institutions by which it was his gracious will that the Chosen People should regulate their lives. The history which he writes is sacred and ecclesiastical rather than secular and civil; his preoccupation is with Israel as a Church rather than as a nation. Hence, while he dwells at comparative length on the lives of the patriarchs and prophets to whom the deity deigned to reveal himself, he hurries over whole generations of common mortals, whom he barely mentions by name, as if they were mere links to connect one religious epoch with another, mere packthread on which to string at rare intervals the splendid jewels of revelation. His attitude to the past is sufficiently explained by the circumstances of the times in which he lived. The great age of Israel was over; its independence was gone, and with it the hopes of worldly prosperity and glory. The rosy dreams of empire, which the splendid reigns of David and Solomon had conjured up in the hearts of the people, and which may have lingered for a while, like morning clouds, even after the disruption of the monarchy, had long ago faded in the clouded evening of the nation's day, under the grim reality of foreign domination. Barred from all the roads of purely mundane ambition, the irrepressible idealism of the national temperament now found a vent for itself in another direction. Its dreams took a different cast. If earth was shut upon it, heaven was still open; and, like Jacob at Bethel, with enemies behind him and before, the dreamer beheld a ladder stretching up beyond the clouds, by which angelic hosts might descend to guard and comfort the forlorn pilgrim. In short, the leaders of Israel sought to console and compensate their nation for the humiliations she had to endure in the secular sphere by raising her to a position of supremacy in the spiritual. For this purpose they constructed or perfected an elaborate system of religious ritual designed to forestall and engross the divine favour, and so to make Zion the holy city, the joy and centre of God's kingdom on earth. With these aims and ambitions the tone of public life became more and more clerical, its interests ecclesiastical, its predominant influence priestly. The king was replaced by the high priest, who succeeded even to the purple robes and golden crown of his predecessor.[1] The revolution which thus substituted a line of pontiffs for a line of temporal rulers at Jerusalem was like that which converted the Rome of the Cæsars into the Rome of the mediæval Popes.

It is this movement of thought, this current of religious aspirations setting strongly in the direction of ecclesiasticism, which is reflected—we may almost say

[1] W. Robertson Smith, *The Old Testament in the Jewish Church*,[2] p. 445.

arrested and crystallized—in the Priestly Code.   The intellectual and moral limitations of the movement are mirrored in the corresponding limitations of the writer. It is the formal side of religion in which alone he is really interested ; it is in the details of rites and ceremonies, of ecclesiastical furniture and garments, that he revels with genuine gusto.   The deeper side of religion is practically a sealed book for him : its moral and spiritual aspects he barely glances at : into the profound problems of immortality and the origin of evil, which have agitated inquiring spirits in all the ages, he never enters.   With his absorption in the minutiæ of ritual, his indifference to purely secular affairs, his predilection for chronology and genealogy, for dates and figures—in a word, for the dry bones rather than the flesh and blood of history—the priestly historian is like one of those monkish chroniclers of the Middle Ages who looked out on the great world through the narrow loophole of a cloistered cell or the many-tinted glass of a cathedral window.   His intellectual horizon was narrowed, the atmosphere in which he beheld events was coloured, by the medium through which he saw them.   Thus the splendours of the Tabernacle in the wilderness, invisible to all eyes but his, are as if they had loomed on his heated imagination through the purple lights of a rose-window or the gorgeous panes of some flamboyant oriel.   Even in the slow processes or sudden catastrophes which have fashioned or transformed the material universe he discerned little more than the signs and wonders vouchsafed by the deity to herald new epochs of religious dispensation.   For him the work of Creation was a grand prelude to the institution of the sabbath.[1]   The vault of heaven itself, spangled with glorious luminaries, was a magnificent dial-plate on which the finger of God pointed eternally to the correct seasons of the feasts in the ecclesiastical calendar.[2]   The Deluge, which swept away almost the whole of mankind, was the occasion which the repentant deity took to establish a covenant with the miserable survivors ; and the rainbow, glowing in iridescent radiance against the murky storm-cloud, was nothing but the divine seal appended to the covenant as a guarantee of its genuine and irrevocable character.[3]   For the priestly historian was a lawyer as well as an ecclesiastic, and as such he took great pains to prove that the friendly relations of God to his people rested on a strictly legal basis, being authenticated by a series of contracts into which both parties entered with all due formality.   He is never so much in his element as when he is expounding these covenants ; he never wearies of recalling the long series of Israel's title-deeds.   Nowhere does this dryasdust antiquary, this rigid ritualist, so sensibly relax his normal severity, nowhere does he so nearly unbend and thaw, as when he is expatiating on the congenial subject of contracts and conveyances.   His masterpiece of historical narrative is acknow-

---

[1] Genesis ii, 1 *sq.*

[2] Genesis i, 14.   The Hebrew word here translated " seasons " (מוֹעֲדִים) " appears never (certainly not in P) to be used of the natural seasons of the year, but always of a time conventionally agreed upon, or fixed by some circumstance.   The commonest application is to the *sacred seasons* of the ecclesiastical year, which are fixed by the moon " (Principal J. Skinner, in his *Critical and Exegetical Commentary on Genesis*, p. 26).

[3] Genesis ix, 8–17.

ledged to be his account of the negotiations into which the widowed Abraham entered with the sons of Heth in order to obtain a family vault in which to bury his wife.[1] The lugubrious nature of the transaction does not damp the professional zest of the narrator; and the picture he has drawn of it combines the touches of no mean artist with the minute exactitude of a practised conveyancer. At this distance of time the whole scene still passes before us, as similar scenes may have passed before the eyes of the writer, and as they may still be witnessed in the East, when two well-bred Arab sheikhs fence dexterously over a point of business, while they observe punctiliously the stately forms and courtesies of Oriental diplomacy. But such pictures are rare indeed in this artist's gallery. Landscapes he hardly attempted, and his portraits are daubs, lacking all individuality, life, and colour. In that of Moses, which he laboured most, the great leader is little more than a lay figure rigged out to distribute ecclesiastical upholstery and millinery.[2]

Very different are the pictures of the patriarchal age bequeathed to us by the author of the Jehovistic document. In purity of outline, lightness and delicacy of touch, and warmth of colouring, they are unsurpassed, perhaps unequalled, in literature. The finest effects are produced by the fewest strokes, because every stroke is that of a master who knows instinctively just what to put in and what to leave out. Thus, while his whole attention seems to be given to the human figures in the foreground, who stand out from the canvas with lifelike truth and solidity, he contrives simultaneously, with a few deft, almost imperceptible touches, to indicate the landscape behind them, and so to complete a harmonious picture which stamps itself indelibly on the memory. The scene, for example, of Jacob and Rachel at the well, with the flocks of sheep lying round it in the noontide heat, is as vivid in the writer's words as it is in the colours of Raphael.

And to this exquisite picturesqueness in the delineation of human life he adds a charming naïvety, an antique simplicity, in his descriptions of the divine. He carries us back to the days of old, when no such awful gulf was supposed to yawn between man and the deity. In his pages we read how God moulded the first man out of clay, as a child shapes its mud baby[3]; how he walked in the garden in the cool of the evening and called to the shamefaced couple who had been hiding behind trees[4]; how he made coats of skin to replace the too scanty fig-leaves of our first parents[5]; how he shut the door behind Noah, when the patriarch had entered into the ark[6]; how he sniffed the sweet savour of the burning sacrifice[7]; how he came down to look at the tower of Babel,[8] apparently because, viewed from the sky, it was beyond his reach of vision; how he conversed with Abraham at the door of his tent, in the heat of the day, under the shadow of the whispering oaks.[9]

[1] Genesis xxiii.
[2] W. Robertson Smith, *The Old Testament in the Jewish Church,*[2] p. 409.
[3] Genesis ii, 7.　　　　　　　　[4] Genesis iii, 8 *sq.*
[5] Genesis iii, 21.　　　　　　　[6] Genesis vii, 16.
[7] Genesis viii, 21.　　　　　　　[8] Genesis xi, 5 and 7.
[9] Genesis xviii, 1 *sqq.* In the English Authorized Version the trees have disappeared from the picture and been replaced by plains. They are rightly restored in the Revised

In short, the whole work of this delightful writer is instinct with a breath of poetry, with something of the freshness and fragrance of the olden time, which invests it with an ineffable and immortal charm.[1]

In the composite narrative of the Great Flood which we possess in Genesis, the separate ingredients contributed by the Jehovistic and the Priestly documents respectively are distinguishable from each other both by verbal and by material differences. To take the verbal differences first, the most striking is that in the Hebrew original the deity is uniformly designated, in the Jehovistic document by the name of *Jehovah* (*Jahweh*), and in the Priestly document by the name of *Elohim*, which in the English version are rendered respectively by the words "Lord" and "God." In representing the Hebrew *Jehovah* (*Jahweh*) by "Lord," the English translators follow the practice of the Jews, who, in reading the Scriptures aloud, uniformly substitute the title *Adonai* or "Lord" for the sacred name of Jehovah, wherever they find the latter written in the text. Hence the English reader may assume as a general rule that in the passages of the English version, where the title "Lord" is applied to the deity, the name Jehovah stands for it in the written or printed Hebrew text.[2] But in the narrative of the Flood

Version, though the correct rendering of the Hebrew word is perhaps rather "terebinths" than "oaks."

[1] As to the two documents, the Jehovistic (J) and the Priestly (P), see W. Robertson Smith, *The Old Testament in the Jewish Church*,[2] pp. 319 *sqq.*, 381 *sqq.*, 442 *sqq.*; J. Estlin Carpenter and G. Harford-Battersby, *The Hexateuch*, i, 33 *sqq.*, 97 *sqq.*, 121 *sqq.*; E. Kautsch, *Die heilige Schrift des Alten Testaments* (Freiburg i. B. und Leipzig, 1894), ii, 150 *sqq.*, 188 *sqq.*; W. H. Bennett, *Genesis*, pp. 9 *sqq.*, 22 *sqq.*, 34 *sqq.*; W. H. Bennett and W. F. Adeney, *A Biblical Introduction*,[5] pp. 20 *sqq.*; S. R. Driver, *Introduction to the Literature of the Old Testament*,[9] pp. 10 *sqq.*, 116 *sqq.*; *id.*, *The Book of Genesis*,[10] Introduction, pp. iv *sqq.*; K. Budde, *Geschichte der althebräischen Litteratur*, pp. 45–65, 183–205; J. Skinner, *Critical and Exegetical Commentary on Genesis*, pp. xxxii–lxvii; H. Gunkel, *Genesis übersetzt und erklärt*[3] (Göttingen, 1910), pp. lxxx *sqq.*, xcii *sqq.*; R. Kittel, *Geschichte des Volkes Israel*[2] (Gotha, 1909–1912), i, 273–333, ii, 398 *sqq.* Critics seem generally to agree that the Priestly Code is the framework into which the three other main constituents of the Hexateuch have been fitted, and that it was substantially "the book of the law of Moses," which was publicly promulgated by Ezra at Jerusalem in 444 B.C. and accepted by the people as the basis of a new reformation (Nehemiah viii). But the work of combining the Priestly Code with the other documents, so as to form our present Hexateuch, appears to have been carried out at a later date, perhaps about 400 B.C. See J. Estlin Carpenter and G. Harford-Battersby, *The Hexateuch*, i, 176 *sqq.*; W. H. Bennett and F. W. Adeney, *op. cit.*, pp. 56 *sqq.* Besides the Priestly Code (P) and the Jehovistic document (J), the two main constituents of the Hexateuch are Deuteronomy (the D of the critics) and the Elohistic document (the E of the critics). Of these, the Elohistic is the older; it is generally believed to have been composed in northern Israel not very long after the Jehovistic document, perhaps early in the eighth century B.C. In style and character it is akin to the Jehovistic document, but the writer is not so great a literary artist, though his religous and moral standpoint is somewhat more advanced. Unlike the Jehovistic writer, he uses the divine name *Elohim* for God instead of Jehovah. It is generally believed that the main part of Deuteronomy is "the book of the law" which was found in the temple at Jerusalem in 621 B.C. and formed the basis of Josiah's reformation (II Kings xxii, 8 *sqq.*). On these matters the reader will find the evidence stated and discussed in the works mentioned at the beginning of this note.

[2] See E. Kautsch, in *Encyclopædia Biblica*, ii, 3320 *sqq.*, *s.v.* "Names

and throughout Genesis the Priestly writer avoids the use of the name Jehovah and substitutes for it the term *Elohim*, which is the ordinary Hebrew word for God; and his reason for doing so is that according to him the divine name Jehovah was first revealed by God to Moses,[1] and therefore could not have been applied to him in the earlier ages of the world. On the other hand, the Jehovistic writer has no such theory as to the revelation of the name Jehovah; hence he bestows it on the deity without scruple from the Creation onwards.

Apart from this capital distinction between the documents, there are verbal differences which do not appear in the English translation. Thus, one set of words is used for " male and female " in the Jehovistic document, and quite a different set in the Priestly.[2] Again, the words translated " destroy " in the English version are different in the two documents,[3] and similarly with the words which the English translators represent by " die "[4] and " dried."[5]

But the material differences between the Jehovistic and the Priestly narratives are still more remarkable, and as they amount in some cases to positive contradictions, the proof that they emanate from separate documents may be regarded as complete. Thus in the Jehovistic narrative the clean animals are distinguished from the unclean, and while seven pairs of every sort of clean animals are admitted to the ark, only one pair of each sort of unclean animals is suffered to enter.[6] On the other hand, the Priestly writer makes no such invidious distinction between the animals, but admits them to the ark on a footing of perfect equality, though at the same time he impartially limits them all alike to a single couple of each sort.[7] The explanation of this discrepancy is that in the view of the Priestly writer the distinction between clean and unclean animals was first revealed by God to Moses,[8] and could not therefore have been known to his predecessor Noah; whereas the Jehovistic writer, untroubled by any such theory, naïvely assumes the distinction between clean and unclean animals to have been familiar to mankind from the earliest times, as if it rested on a natural difference too obvious to be overlooked by anybody.

Another serious discrepancy between the two writers relates to the duration of the Flood. In the Jehovistic narrative the rain lasted forty days and forty nights,[9] and afterwards Noah passed three weeks in the ark before the water had

---

[1] Exodus vi, 2 *sq.*

[2] אִישׁ וְאִשְׁתּוֹ in J (vii, 2), זָכָר וּנְקֵבָה in P (vi, 19, vii, 9, 16).

[3] מָחָה in J (vi, 7, vii, 4, 23), שָׁחַת in P (vi, 13, 17, ix, 11, 15). The former word means properly " blot out," as it is rendered in the margin of the English Revised Version; the latter is the ordinary Hebrew word for " destroy."

[4] מוּת in J (vii, 22), גָּוַע in P (vi, 17, vii, 21). The former is the ordinary Hebrew word or " die "; the latter is sometimes translated " give up the ghost."

[5] חָרֵב in J (viii, 13), יָבֵשׁ in P (viii, 14). All the foregoing and other verbal differences between the two documents are noted by Principal J. Skinner in his *Critical and Exegetical Commentary on Genesis*, p. 148. Compare H. Gunkel, *Genesis übersetzt und erklärt*[3] (Göttingen, 1910), p. 138.

[6] Genesis vii, 2, compare viii, 20.

[7] Genesis vi, 19 *sq.*, vii, 15 *sq.*

[8] Leviticus xi; Deuteronomy xiv, 4–20.

[9] Genesis vii, 12, 17.

subsided enough to let him land.[1]   On this reckoning the Flood lasted sixty-one days.   On the other hand, in the Priestly narrative it was a hundred and fifty days before the water began to sink,[2] and the Flood lasted altogether for twelve months and eleven days.[3]   As the Hebrew months were lunar, twelve of them would amount to three hundred and fifty-four days, and eleven days added to them would give a solar year of three hundred and sixty-five days.[4]   Since the Priestly writer thus assigns to the duration of the Flood the precise length of a solar year, we may safely assume that he lived at a time when the Jews were able to correct the serious error of the lunar calendar by observation of the sun.

Again, the two writers differ from each other in the causes which they allege for the Flood; for whereas the Jehovistic writer puts it down to rain only,[5] the Priestly writer speaks of subterranean waters bursting forth as well as of sheets of water descending from heaven.[6]

Lastly, the Jehovistic writer represents Noah as building an altar and sacrificing to God in gratitude for his escape from the Flood.[7]   The Priestly writer, on the other hand, makes no mention either of the altar or of the sacrifice ; no doubt because from the standpoint of the Levitical law, which he occupied, there could be no legitimate altar anywhere but in the temple at Jerusalem, and because for a mere layman like Noah to offer a sacrifice would have been an unheard-of impropriety, a gross encroachment on the rights of the clergy which he could not for a moment dream of imputing to the respectable patriarch.

Thus a comparison of the Jehovistic and the Priestly narratives strongly confirms the conclusion of the critics that the two were originally independent, and that the Jehovistic is considerably the older.   For the Jehovistic writer is clearly ignorant of the law of the one sanctuary, which forbade the offering of sacrifice anywhere but at Jerusalem ; and as that law was first clearly enunciated and enforced by King Josiah in 621 b.c., it follows that the Jehovistic document must have been composed some time, probably a long time, before that date.   For a like reason the Priestly document must have been composed some time, probably a long time, after that date, since the writer implicitly recognizes the law of the one sanctuary by refusing to impute a breach of it to Noah.   Thus, whereas the Jehovistic writer betrays a certain archaic simplicity in artlessly attributing to the earliest ages of the world the religious institutions and phraseology of his own time, the Priestly writer reveals the reflection of a later age, which has worked out a definite theory of religious evolution and applies it rigidly to history.

A very cursory comparison of the Hebrew with the Babylonian account of the Deluge may suffice to convince that the two narratives are not independent, but that one of them must be derived from the other, or both from a common original.

---

[1] Genesis viii, 6–13.   [2] Genesis viii, 3.

[3] Genesis vii, 11, compared with viii, 14.

[4] S. R. Driver, *The Book of Genesis*,[10] p. 85 ; J. Skinner, *Critical and Exegetical Commentary on Genesis*, pp. 167 *sqq.* ; H. Gunkel, *Genesis übersetzt und erklärt*,[3] pp. 146 *sq.*

[5] Genesis vii, 12.   [6] Genesis vii, 11, compare viii, 2.

[7] Genesis viii, 20 *sq.*

The points of resemblance between the two are far too numerous and detailed to be accidental. In both narratives the divine powers resolve to destroy mankind by a great flood; in both the secret is revealed beforehand to a man by a god, who directs him to build a great vessel, in which to save himself and seed of every kind. It is probably no mere accidental coincidence that in the Babylonian story, as reported by Berosus, the hero saved from the Flood was the *tenth* King of Babylon, and that in the Hebrew story Noah was the *tenth* man in descent from Adam. In both narratives the favoured man, thus warned of God, builds a huge vessel in several stories, makes it water-tight with pitch or bitumen, and takes into it his family and animals of all sorts: in both, the Deluge is brought about in large measure by heavy rain, and lasts for a greater or less number of days: in both, all mankind are drowned except the hero and his family: in both, the man sends forth birds, a raven and a dove, to see whether the water of the Flood has abated: in both, the dove after a time returns to the ship because it could find no place in which to rest: in both, the raven does not return: in both, the vessel at last grounds on a mountain: in both, the hero, in gratitude for his rescue, offers sacrifice on the mountain: in both, the gods smell the sweet savour, and their anger is appeased.

So much for the general resemblance between the Babylonian narrative as a whole, and the Hebrew narrative as a whole. But if we take into account the separate elements of the Hebrew narrative we shall see that the Jehovistic narrative is in closer agreement than the Priestly with the Babylonian. Alike in the Jehovistic and in the Babylonian narrative special prominence is given to the number seven. In the Jehovistic version, Noah has a seven days' warning of the coming Deluge: he takes seven pairs of every sort of clean animals with him into the ark: he allows intervals of seven days to elapse between the successive despatches of the dove from the ark. In the Babylonian version the Flood lasts at its greatest height for seven days; and the hero sets out the sacrificial vessels by sevens on the mountain. Again, alike in the Jehovistic and the Babylonian version, special mention is made of shutting the door of the ship or ark when the man, his family, and the animals have entered into it; in both alike we have the picturesque episode of sending forth the raven and the dove from the vessel, and in both alike the offering of the sacrifice, the smelling of it by the gods, and their consequent appeasement. On the other hand, in certain particulars the Priestly narrative in Genesis approaches more closely than the Jehovistic to the Babylonian. Thus, in both the Priestly and the Babylonian version exact directions are given for the construction of the vessel: in both alike it is built in several stories, each of which is divided into numerous cabins: in both alike it is made watertight by being caulked with pitch or bitumen: in both alike it grounds on a mountain; and in both alike, on issuing from the vessel, the hero receives the divine blessing.

But if the Hebrew and Babylonian narratives are closely related to each other, how is the relation to be explained? The Babylonian cannot be derived from the Hebrew, since it is older than the Hebrew by at least eleven or twelve centuries.

Moreover, "as Zimmern has remarked, the very essence of the Biblical narrative presupposes a country liable, like Babylonia, to inundations; so that it cannot be doubted that the story was 'indigenous in Babylonia, and transplanted to Palestine.'"[1]   But if the Hebrews derived the story of the Great Flood from Babylonia, when and how did they do so? We have no information on the subject, and the question can only be answered conjecturally. Some scholars of repute have supposed that the Jews first learned the legend in Babylon during the captivity, and that the Biblical narrative is consequently not older than the sixth century before our era.[2] This view might be tenable if we only possessed the Hebrew version of the deluge legend in the Priestly recension; for the Priestly Code, as we saw, was probably composed during or after the captivity, and it is perfectly possible that the writers of it acquired a knowledge of the Babylonian tradition either orally or from Babylonian literature during their exile or perhaps after their return to Palestine; for it is reasonable to suppose that the intimate relations which the conquest established between the two countries may have led to a certain diffusion of Babylonian literature in Palestine, and of Jewish literature in Babylonia. On this view some of the points in which the Priestly narrative departs from the Jehovistic and approximates to the Babylonian may conceivably have been borrowed directly by the Priestly writers from Babylonian sources. Such points are the details as to the construction of the ark, and in particular the smearing of it with pitch or bitumen, which is a characteristic product of Babylonia.[3] But that the Hebrews were acquainted with the story of the Great Flood, and that too in a form closely akin to the Babylonian, long before they were carried away into captivity, is abundantly proved by the Jehovistic narrative in Genesis, which may well date from the ninth century before our era and can hardly be later than the eighth.

Assuming, then, that the Hebrews in Palestine were familiar from an early time with the Babylonian legend of the Deluge, we have still to ask, how and when did they learn it? Two answers to the question have been given. On the one hand, it has been held that the Hebrews may have brought the legend with them, when they migrated from Babylonia to Palestine about two thousand years before Christ.[4] On the other hand, it has been suggested that, after their settlement in Palestine, the Hebrews may have borrowed the story from the native Canaanites, who in their turn may have learned it through the medium of Babylonian literature some time in

[1] S. R. Driver, *The Book of Genesis*[10], p. 107.

[2] This is, or was, the opinion of P. Haupt and Fr. Delitsch, as reported by E. Schrader, *The Cuneiform Inscriptions and the Old Testament*, i, 55. The view is rightly rejected by Schrader.

[3] Herodotus, i, 179, with the note in George Rawlinson's translation (Fourth Edition, vol. i, London, 1880, p. 300).

[4] This is the view of Professor M. Jastrow (*Hebrew and Babylonian Traditions*, pp. 13 *sqq.*), who identifies Abraham's contemporary, Amraphel, King of Shinar (Genesis xiv, 1), with Hammurabi, King of Babylon, thus dating Abraham and his migration from Babylonia to Palestine about the beginning of the second millenium B.C. As to Hammurabi's date, see above, p. 244, note [1].

the second millennium before our era.[1] Which, if either, of these views is the true one, we have at present no means of deciding.

It has been proposed to explain the Babylonian and Hebrew traditions of a great flood by the inundations to which the lower valley of the Euphrates and Tigris is annually exposed by the heavy rains and melting snows in the mountains of Armenia. " The basis of the story," we are told, " is the yearly phenomenon of the rainy and stormy season, which lasts in Babylonia for several months, and during which time whole districts in the Euphrates Valley are submerged. Great havoc was caused by the rains and storms until the perfection of canal systems regulated the overflow of the Euphrates and Tigris, when what had been a curse was converted into a blessing, and brought about that astonishing fertility for which Babylonia became famous. The Hebrew story of the Deluge recalls a particularly destructive season that had made a profound impression, and the comparison with the parallel story found on clay tablets of Ashurbanipal's library confirms this view of the local setting of the tale."[2] In favour of this view it may be said that in the Babylonian and the oldest form of the Hebrew tradition the cause of the Deluge is said to have been heavy rain.[3] The theory may also be supported by the dangerous inundations to which the country is still yearly liable through the action of the same natural causes. When Loftus, the first excavator of the ancient city of Erech, arrived in Bagdad on the 5th of May, 1849, he found the whole population in a state of the utmost apprehension and alarm. In consequence of the rapid melting of the snows on the Kurdish mountains, and the enormous influx of water from the Euphrates through the Seglawiyya canal, the Tigris had risen that spring to the unprecedented height of twenty-two and a half feet, which was about five feet above its highest level in ordinary years and exceeded the great rise of 1831, when the river broke down the walls and destroyed no less than seven thousand dwellings in a single night, at a time when the plague was committing the most fearful ravages among the inhabitants. A few days before the arrival of the English party, the Turkish pasha of Bagdad had summoned the whole population, as one man, to guard against the general danger by raising a strong high mound completely round the walls. Mats of reeds were placed outside to bind the earth compactly together. The water was thus prevented from devastating the interior of the city, though it filtered through the fine alluvial soil and stood several feet deep in the cellars. Outside the city it reached to within two feet of the top of the bank. On the side of the river the houses alone, many of them very old and frail, prevented the ingress of the flood. It was a critical

---

[1] H. Gressmann, in *Das Gilgamesch-Epos übersetzt und erklärt*, von A. Ungnad und H. Gressmann, p. 220. On this theory, see Principal J. Skinner, *Critical and Exegetical Commentary on Genesis*, p. x, who objects to it that "there are no recognizable traces of a specifically Canaanite medium having been interposed between the Babylonian originals and the Hebrew accounts of the Creation and the Flood, such as we may surmise in the case of the Paradise myth."

[2] M. Jastrow *Hebrew and Babylonian Traditions*, pp. 37 *sq.* ; compare *id.*, pp. 322 *sq.*

[3] Above, pp. 239, 243, 245, 256.

juncture. Men were stationed night and day to watch the barriers. If the dam or any of the foundations had failed, Bagdad must have been bodily washed away. Happily the pressure was withstood, and the inundation gradually subsided. The country on all sides for miles was under water, so that there was no possibility of proceeding beyond the dyke, except in the boats which were established as ferries to keep up communication across the flood. The city was for a time an island in a vast inland sea, and it was a full month before the inhabitants could ride beyond the walls. As the summer advanced, the presence of the stagnant water caused malaria to such an extent that, out of a population of seventy thousand, no less than twelve thousand died of fever.[1]

If the floods caused by the melting of the snow in the Armenian mountains can thus endanger the cities in the river valley down to modern times, it is reasonable to suppose that they did so in antiquity also, and that the Babylonian tradition of the destruction of the city of Shurippak in such an inundation may be well founded. It is true that the city appears to have ultimately perished by fire rather than by water;[2] but this is quite consistent with the supposition that at some earlier time it had been destroyed by a flood and afterwards rebuilt.

However, the theory which would explain the Babylonian and Hebrew tradition of a great flood by the inundations to which the country is annually exposed, may be combated by an argument drawn from the analogy of Egypt. For Egypt from time immemorial has been similarly subject to yearly inundations; yet it has never, so far as we know, either evolved a flood legend of its own or accepted the flood legend of its great Oriental rival. If annual floods sufficed to produce the legend in Babylonia, why, it may be asked, did not the same cause produce the same effect in Egypt?

To meet this difficulty a different explanation of the Babylonian story has been put forward in recent years by an eminent geologist, Professor Eduard Suess of Vienna. Regarding the regular annual changes in the basin of the Euphrates as insufficient to account for the legend, he has recourse to irregular or catastrophic causes. He points out that "there are other peculiarities of the Euphrates valley which may occasionally tend to exacerbate the evils attendant on the inundations. It is very subject to seismic disturbances; and the ordinary consequences of a sharp earthquake shock might be seriously complicated by its effect on a broad sheet of water. Moreover the Indian Ocean lies within the region of typhoons; and if, at the height of an inundation, a hurricane from the south-east swept up the Persian Gulf, driving its shallow waters upon the delta and damming back the outflow, perhaps for hundreds of miles up-stream, a diluvial catastrophe, fairly up to the mark of Hasisadra's, might easily result."[3]

---

[1] W. K. Loftus, *Travels and Researches in Chaldæa and Susiana* (London, 1857), pp. 7 *sq.*

[2] Above, p. 246.

[3] T. H. Huxley, "Hasisadra's Adventure," *Collected Essays*, iv, 246 *sq.* Thus clearly and concisely does Huxley sum up the theory which Professor E. Suess expounds at great length in his work, *The Face of the Earth*, vol. i (Oxford, 1904), pp. 17–72.

In support of his catastrophic theory Professor Suess appeals to two features in the Hebrew version of the flood story, or rather to one feature which actually occurs in that version, and to another which he would import into it by altering the text so as to suit his hypothesis. We will consider each of his arguments separately.

In the first place Professor Suess points out that in the Hebrew narrative one cause alleged for the Deluge is the breaking out of subterranean waters.[1] " This rising of great quantities of water from the deep," he says, " is a phenomenon which is a characteristic accompaniment of earthquakes in the alluvial districts of great rivers. The subterranean water is contained in the recent deposits of the great plains on both sides of the stream, and its upper limit rises to right and left above the mean level of the river, its elevation increasing in proportion to the distance from the river. What lies beneath this limit is saturated and mobile ; the ground above it is dry and friable. When seismic oscillations occur in a district of this kind the brittle upper layer of the ground splits open in long clefts, and from these fissures the underground water, either clear or as a muddy mass, is violently ejected, sometimes in great volumes, sometimes in isolated jets several yards high."[2] For example, the young alluvial land about the Danube in Wallachia was rent by an earthquake in 1838, and from the fissures water spouted out in many places fathoms high. The same thing happened when the alluvial plain of the Mississippi, a little below the confluence of the Ohio, was convulsed by an earthquake in January, 1812 : the water that had filled the subterranean cavities forced a passage for itself and blew up the earth with loud explosions, throwing up an enormous quantity of carbonized wood in jets from ten to fifteen feet high, while at the same time the surface of the ground sank, and a black liquid rose as high as a horse's belly. Again, in January, 1862, a violent shock of earthquake affected the whole region south of Lake Baikal, and in particular the delta of the river Selenga which flows into the lake. In the town of Kudara the wooden lids of the fountains were shot into the air like corks from champagne bottles, and springs of tepid water rose in places to a height of more than twenty feet. So terrified were the Mongols that they caused the Lamas to perform ceremonies to appease the evil spirits which, as they imagined, were shaking the earth.[3]

On this it is to be observed that the reference to subterranean waters as one cause of the Deluge occurs only in the Hebrew version of the legend, and even there it is found only in the later Priestly narrative : it does not occur in the earlier Jehovistic narrative, nor in the still earlier Babylonian version[4]; nor, finally,

---

[1] Genesis vii, 11 ; viii, 2.

[2] E. Suess, *The Face of the Earth*, i, 31.

[3] E. Suess, *The Face of the Earth*, i, 31 *sq.*

[4] Professor Suess, indeed, discovers a reference to subterranean waters in a passage of the Babylonian legend which, following Professor Paul Haupt, he translates " the Anunnaki caused floods to rise," supposing the Anunnaki to be " the spirits of the deep, of the great subterranean waters " (*The Face of the Earth*, i, 31). But the better translation of that passage seems to be, " the Anunnaki lifted up flaming torches " (so P. Jensen, A. Jeremias, L. W. King, W. Muss

is it found in the original Sumerian legend from which both the Babylonian and the Hebrew stories are derived. Accordingly it may be dismissed as a late addition to the legend on which it would be unsafe to build any hypothesis.

But Professor Suess appeals to the Hebrew narrative for another argument in favour of his view that the Deluge was caused principally by a great sea-wave driven up from the Persian Gulf by the combined force of an earthquake and a typhoon. This he is enabled to do by altering the Hebrew text of Genesis in two passages so as to yield the meaning "the flood from the sea" instead of "the flood of waters."[1] The textual change, it is true, is very slight, for it extends only to the vowel-points and leaves the consonants unaffected. But though the vowel-points form no part of the original Hebrew text of the Scriptures, having been introduced into it not earlier than the sixth century of our era, they are not to be lightly altered, since they represent the traditional pronunciation of the sacred words, as it had been handed down with scrupulous care, generation after generation, by a guild of technically trained scholars, the Massorets, as they were called, who "devoted themselves to preserving not only the exact writing of the received consonantal text, but the exact pronunciation and even the musical cadence proper to every word of the sacred text, according to the rules of the synagogal chanting."[2] Hence the proposed emendation in the two verses of Genesis has been rightly rejected by the best recent scholars,[3] and with it the appeal to the Hebrew text for evidence of the marine origin of the great flood must be dismissed as unfounded.

It does not of course follow that Professor Suess's explanation of the Babylonian Deluge is false because the arguments in favour of it which he deduces from the Biblical narrative carry little or no weight. If that narrative, as seems probable, rests on a basis of fact, it is quite possible that the Great Flood which it describes may actually have been produced by an earthquake or a typhoon, or by both combined. But the theory that it was so produced derives extremely little support from the only authorities open to us, the Hebrew, Babylonian, and Sumerian traditions; hence it hardly amounts to more than a plausible conjecture. On a simple calculation of chances, it seems more likely that the catastrophe was brought about by forces which are known to act regularly every year on the Euphrates valley, and to be quite capable of producing widespread inundations, rather than by assumed forces which, though certainly capable of causing

Arnolt, M. Jastrow, P. Dhorme, A. Ungnad, R. W. Rogers). Hence the reference must be to some phenomena, not of water, but of light, perhaps to flashes of lightning, as Jensen and Dhorme suggest (see P. Jensen, *Assyrisch-Babylonische Mythen und Epen*, p. 580; P. Dhorme, *Choix de Textes Religieux Assyro-Babyloniens*, p. 110).

[1] Genesis vi, 17, and vii, 6, reading מִיָּם for מַיִם (*miyam* for *mayim*).

[2] W. Robertson Smith, *The Old Testament in the Jewish Church*[2] (London and Edinburgh, 1892), p. 58. As to the Massorets and their work, see W. R. Smith, *op. cit.*, pp. 58–60.

[3] A. Dillmann and J. Skinner, in their commentaries, explicitly; S. R. Driver and W. H. Bennett, in their commentaries, implicitly. In his critical edition of the Hebrew text (*Biblia Hebraica*, Part i, Leipsic, 1905, p. 8) R. Kittel rejects מַיִם as a gloss.

disastrous floods, are not positively known to have ever acted on the region in question; for, apart from the supposed references in Semitic tradition, I am aware of no record of a Babylonian deluge caused either by an earthquake wave or by a typhoon.

§4. Ancient Greek Stories of a Great Flood.

Legends of a destructive deluge, in which the greater part of mankind perished, meet us in the literature of ancient Greece. As told by the mythographer Apollodorus the story runs thus : "Deucalion was the son of Prometheus. He reigned as king in the country about Phthia and married Pyrrha, the daughter of Epimetheus and Pandora, the first woman fashioned by the gods. But when Zeus wished to destroy the men of the Bronze Age, Deucalion by the advice of Prometheus constructed a chest or ark, and having stored in it what was needful he entered into it with his wife. But Zeus poured a great rain from the sky upon the earth and washed down the greater part of Greece, so that all men perished except a few, who fled to the high mountains near. Then the mountains in Thessaly were parted, and all the world beyond the Isthmus and Peloponnese was overwhelmed. But Deucalion in the ark, floating over the sea for nine days and as many nights, grounded on Parnassus, and there, when the rain ceased, he disembarked and sacrificed to Zeus, the God of Escape. And Zeus sent Hermes to him and allowed him to choose what he would, and he chose men. So Zeus bade him pick up stones and throw them over his head; and the stones which Deucalion threw became men, and the stones which Pyrrha threw became women. That is why in Greek people are called *laoi* from *laas*, 'a stone.'"[1]

In this form the Greek legend is not older than about the middle of the second century before our era, the time when Apollodorus wrote, but in substance it is much more ancient, for the story was told by Hellanicus, a Greek historian of the fifth century B.C., who said that Deucalion's ark drifted not to Parnassus but to Mount Othrys in Thessaly.[2] The other version has the authority of Pindar, who wrote earlier than Hellanicus in the fifth century B.C.; for the poet speaks of Deucalion and Pyrrha descending from Parnassus and creating the human race afresh out of stones.[3] According to some, the first city which they founded after the great flood was Opus, situated in the fertile Locrian plain between the mountains and the Euboic Gulf. But Deucalion is reported to have dwelt at Cynus, the port of Opus, distant a few miles across the plain; and there his wife's tomb was shown to travellers down to the beginning of our era. Her husband's dust is said to have rested at Athens.[4] The coast of Locris, thus associated with

---

[1] Apollodorus, *Bibliotheca*, i, 7, 2.

[2] Scholiast on Pindar, *Olymp.*, ix, 64 ; *Fragmenta Historicorum Graecorum*, ed. C. Müller, i, 48.

[3] Pindar, *Olymp.*, ix, 64 *sqq*.

[4] Strabo, ix, 4, 2, p. 425, ed. Casaubon.

traditions of the Great Flood, is rich in natural beauties.   The road runs at the foot of the mountains, which are of soft and lovely outlines, for the most part covered with forest; while the low hills and glades by the sea are wooded with pines, plane-trees, myrtles, lentisks, and other trees and shrubs, their luxuriant verdure fed by abundant springs.   Across the blue waters of the gulf the eye roams to the island of Euboea, with its winding shores and long line of finely cut mountains standing out against the sky.   The home of Deucalion was on a promontory running out into the gulf.   On it, and on the isthmus which joins it to the land, may still be seen the mouldering ruins of Cynus: a line of fortification walls, built of sandstone, runs round the edge of the height, and the summit is crowned by the remains of a mediæval tower.   The ground is littered with ancient potsherds.[1]

It is said that an ancient city on Parnassus was overwhelmed by the rains which caused the deluge, but the inhabitants, guided by the howling of wolves, found their way to the peaks of the mountain, and when the flood had subsided they descended and built a new city which they called Lycorea or Wolf-town in gratitude for the guidance of the wolves.[2]   Lucian speaks of Deucalion's ark, with the solitary survivors of the human race, grounding on what was afterwards the site of Wolf-town, while as yet all the rest of the world was submerged.[3]   But according to another account, the mountain to which Deucalion escaped was a peak in Argolis, which was afterwards called Nemea after the cattle which cropped the greensward on its grassy slopes.   There the hero built an altar in honour of Zeus the Deliverer, who had delivered him from the Great Flood.[4]   The mountain on which he is said to have alighted is probably the table-mountain, now called Phouka, whose broad flat top towers high above the neighbouring hills, and forms a conspicuous landmark viewed from the plain of Argos.[5]

The Megarians told how in Deucalion's flood Megarus, son of Zeus, escaped by swimming to the top of Mount Gerania, being guided by the cries of some cranes, which flew over the rising waters and from which the mountain afterwards received its new name.[6]   According to Aristotle, writing in the fourth century B.C., the ravages of the deluge in Deucalion's time were felt most sensibly " in ancient Hellas, which is the country about Dodona and the River Achelous, for that river has changed its bed in many places.   In those days the land was inhabited by the Selli and the people who were then called Greeks (*Graikoi*) but are now named

[1] Ludwig Ross, *Wanderungen in Griechenland* (Halle, 1851), i, 94 *sq.*

[2] Pausanias, x, 6, 2.

[3] Lucian, *Timon*, 3.   Elsewhere he refers to the ark and to the creation of men out of stones (*De Saltatione*, 39).

[4] *Etymologicum Magnum*, p. 176, *s.v.* Ἀφέσιος, referring to the Second Book of Arrian's *Bithyniaca.*

[5] The modern *Phouka* seems to be the Apesas of the ancients (Pausanias, ii, 5, 3, with the note in my commentary), which again seems to be connected with Zeus *Aphesios* (Deliverer), to whom Deucalion built an altar on the mountain.

[6] Pausanias, i, 40, 1 (Gerania from *geranoi*, " cranes ").

Hellenes."[1] Some people thought that the sanctuary at Dodona was founded by Deucalion and Pyrrha, who dwelt among the Molossians of that country.[2] In the fourth century B.C., Plato also mentions, without describing, the flood which took place in the time of Deucalion and Pyrrha, and he represents the Egyptian priests as ridiculing the Greeks for believing that there had been only one deluge, whereas there had been many.[3] The Parian chronicler, who drew up his chronological table in the year 265 B.C.,[4] dated Deucalion's flood one thousand two hundred and sixty-five years before his own time[5]; according to this calculation the cataclysm occurred in the year 1539 B.C.

At a later age the Roman poet Ovid decked out the tradition of the Great Flood in the pinchbeck rhetoric which betrayed the decline of literary taste. He tells us that Jupiter, weary of the wickedness and impiety of the men of the Iron Age, resolved to destroy the whole of mankind at one fell swoop. His first idea was to overwhelm them under the flaming thunderbolts which he brandished in his red right hand; but on reflection he laid these dangerous weapons aside, lest the upper air and heaven itself should catch fire from the great conflagration which they would kindle on earth; and in this prudent resolution he was confirmed by an imperfect recollection of an old prophecy that the whole world, sky and earth alike, was destined to perish in a grand and final combustion. Accordingly he decided on the safer course of turning on the celestial taps and drowning the whole wicked race under the tremendous shower bath. So he shut up the North Wind in the cave of Aeolus, to prevent him from sweeping the murky clouds from the blue sky, and he let loose the South Wind, who flew abroad rigged out in all the stage properties calculated to strike terror into the beholder. He flapped his dripping wings: his dreadful face was veiled in pitchy blackness: mists sat on his forehead, his beard was soaking wet, and water ran down from his hoary hair. In his train the sky lowered, thunder crashed, and the rainbow shone in spangled glory against the dark rain-clouds. To help the sky-god in his onslaught on mankind his sea-blue brother Neptune summoned an assembly of the rivers and bade them roll in flood over the land, while he himself fetched the earth a smashing blow with his trident, causing it to quake like a jelly. The fountains of the great deep were now opened. The deluge poured over the fields and meadows, whirling away trees, cattle, men and houses. Far and wide nothing was to be seen but a shoreless sea of tossing turbid water. The farmer now rowed in a shallop over the field where he had lately guided the oxen at the plough-tail, and peering down he could discern his crops and the roof of his farmhouse submerged under the waves. He dropped his anchor on a green meadow, his keel grated on

---

[1] Aristotle, *Meteorolog.*, i, 14, p. 352, ed. Im. Bekker (Berlin, 1831).

[2] Plutarch, *Pyrrhus*, 1.

[3] Plato, *Timaeus* pp. 22A, 23B.

[4] L. Ideler, *Handbuch der mathematischen und technischen Chronologie* (Berlin, 1825–6), i 380 *sqq.*

[5] *Marmor Parium*, 6 *sqq.*, in *Fragmenta Historicorum Graecorum*, ed. C. Müller, i, 542.

his own vineyard, and he fished for trout on the tops of the tall elms. Seals now lolled and sprawled where goats had lately nibbled the herbage, and dolphins gambolled and plunged in the woods. When at last nothing remained above the waste of waters but the two peaks of Parnassus, toppling over the heaving billows and reaching up above the clouds, Deucalion and his wife drifted in a little boat to the mountain, and landing adored the nymphs of the Corycian cave and the prophetic goddess Themis, who managed the business of the oracle before it was taken over by Apollo. A righteous and god-fearing man was Deucalion, and his wife was just such another. Touched with compassion at the sight of the honest pair, the sole survivors of so many thousands, Jupiter now dispersed the clouds and the deluge, revealing the blue sky and the green earth to each other once more. So Neptune also laid aside his trident, and summoning the bugler Triton, his back blue with the growth of the purple-shell, he ordered him to sound the " Retire." The bugler obeyed, and putting the shell to his lips he blew from his puffed cheeks such a blast that at the sound of it all the waves and rivers fell back and left the land high and dry. This was all very well, but what were Deucalion and Pyrrha to do now, left solitary in a desolated world, where not a sound broke the dreadful silence save the melancholy lapping of the waves on the lonely shore ? They shed some natural tears, and then wiping them away they resolved to consult the oracle. So pacing sadly by the yellow turbid waters of the Cephisus they repaired to the temple of the goddess. The sacred edifice presented a melancholy spectacle, its walls still overgrown with moss and sea-weed, its courts still deep in slime ; and naturally no fire flamed or smouldered on the defiled altars. However, the goddess was fortunately at home, and in reply to the anxious inquiries of the two suppliants she instructed them, as soon as they had quitted the temple, to veil their heads, unloose their robes, and throw behind their backs the bones of their great parent. This strange answer bewildered them, and for a long time they remained silent. Pyrrha was the first to find her voice, and when at last she broke silence it was to declare respectfully but firmly that nothing would induce her to insult her mother's ghost by flinging her bones about. Her husband, more discerning, said that perhaps by their great parent the goddess meant them to understand the earth, and that by her bones she signified the rocks and stones embedded in the ground. They were not very hopeful of success, but, nothing else occurring to them to do, they decided to make the attempt. So they carried out the instructions of the oracle to the letter, and sure enough the stones which Deucalion threw turned into men, and the stones which Pyrrha threw turned into women. Thus was the earth repeopled after the great flood.[1]

Anyone who compares the laboured ingenuity of this account of the Deluge with the majestic simplicity of the corresponding narrative in Genesis is in a

---

[1] Ovid, *Metamorphoses*, i, 125–415. The fish sticking in the tops of the elms are borrowed from Horace (*Odes*, i, 9 *sq.*).

position to measure the gulf which divides great literature from its tinsel imitation.

In his account of the catastrophe Ovid so far followed ancient Greek tradition as to represent Deucalion and Pyrrha landing on the peak of Parnassus. Later Roman writers carried the pair much farther afield; one of them landed the voyagers on Mount Athos,[1] and another conveyed them as far as Mount Etna.[2]

Various places in Greece, as we have seen, claimed the honour of having been associated in a particular manner with Deucalion and the Great Flood. Among the claimants, as might have been expected, were the Athenians, who, pluming themselves on the vast antiquity from which they had inhabited the land of Attica, had no mind to be left out in the cold when it came to a question of Deucalion and the Deluge. They annexed him accordingly by the simple expedient of alleging that when the clouds gathered dark on Parnassus and the rain came down in torrents on Lycorea, where Deucalion reigned as king, he fled for safety to Athens, and on his arrival founded a sanctuary of Rainy Zeus, and offered thank-offerings for his escape.[3] In this brief form of the legend there is no mention of a ship, and we seem to be left to infer that the hero escaped on foot. Be that as it may, he is said to have founded the old sanctuary of Olympian Zeus, and to have been buried in the city. Down to the second century of our era the local Athenian guides pointed with patriotic pride to the grave of the Greek Noah near the later and far statelier temple of Olympian Zeus, whose ruined columns, towering in solitary grandeur above the modern city, still attract the eye from far, and bear silent but eloquent witness to the glories of ancient Greece.[4]

Nor was this all that the guides had to show in memory of the tremendous cataclysm. Within the great precinct overshadowed by the vast temple of Olympian Zeus they led the curious traveller to a smaller precinct of Olympian Earth, where they pointed to a cleft in the ground a cubit wide. Down that cleft, they assured him, the waters of the Deluge ran away, and down it every year they threw cakes of wheaten meal kneaded with honey.[5] These cakes would seem to have been soul-cakes destined for the consumption of the poor souls who perished in the Great Flood; for we know that a commemoration service or requiem mass was celebrated every year at Athens in their honour. It was called the Festival of the Water-bearing,[6] which suggests that charitable people not only threw cakes but poured water down the cleft in the ground to slake the thirst as well as to stay the hunger of the ghosts in the nether world.

---

[1] Servius, on Virgil, *Bucol.*, vi, 41. [2] Hyginus, *Fabulae*, 153.

[3] *Marmor Parium*, 6 *sq.*, in *Fragmenta Historicorum Graecorum*, ed. C. Müller, i, 542.

[4] Pausanias, i, 18, 8. The tomb of Deucalion at Athens is mentioned also by Strabo, ix, 4, 2, p. 425.

[5] Pausanias, i, 18, 7.

[6] Plutarch, *Sulla*, 14; *Etymologicum Magnum*, p. 774, *s.v.* ὑδροφορία; Hesychius, *s.v.* ὑδροφόρια. The festival fell at the new moon in the month of Anthesterion (Plutarch, *l.c.*). Compare Schol. on Aristophanes, *Acharnians*, 1076, and on *Frogs*, 218; August Mommsen, *Feste der Stadt Athen im Altertum* (Leipsic, 1898), pp. 424 *sq.*

Another place where the Great Flood was commemorated by a similar ceremony was Hierapolis on the Euphrates. There down to the second century of our era the ancient Semitic deities were worshipped in the old way under a transparent disguise imposed on them, like modern drapery on ancient statues, by the nominally Greek civilization which the conquests of Alexander had spread over the East. Chief among these aboriginal divinities was the great Syrian goddess Astarte, who to her Greek worshippers masqueraded under the name of Hera. Lucian has bequeathed to us a very valuable description of the sanctuary and the strange rites performed in it.[1] He tells us that according to the general opinion the sanctuary was founded by Deucalion, in whose time the Great Flood took place. This gives Lucian occasion to relate the Greek story of the Deluge, which according to him ran as follows. The present race of men, he says, are not the first of human kind; there was another race which perished wholly. We are of the second breed, which multiplied after the time of Deucalion. As for the folk before the Flood, it is said that they were exceedingly wicked and lawless; for they neither kept their oaths, nor gave hospitality to strangers, nor respected suppliants, wherefore the great calamity befell them. So the fountains of the deep were opened, and the rain descended in torrents, the rivers swelled, and the sea spread far over the land, till there was nothing but water, water everywhere, and all men perished. But Deucalion was the only man who, by reason of his prudence and piety, survived and formed the link between the first and the second race of men; and the way in which he was saved was this. He had a great ark, and into it he entered with his wives and children; and as he was entering there came to him pigs, and horses, and lions, and serpents, and all other land animals, all of them in pairs. He received them all, and they did him no harm; nay, by God's help there was a great friendship between them, and they all sailed in one ark so long as the flood prevailed on the earth. Such, says Lucian, is the Greek story of Deucalion's deluge; but the people of Hierapolis, he goes on, tell a marvellous thing. They say that a great chasm opened in their country, and all the water of the flood ran away down it. And when that happened, Deucalion built altars and founded a holy temple of Hera beside the chasm. " I have seen the chasm," he proceeds, " and a very small one it is under the temple. Whether it was large of old and has been reduced to its present size in course of time I know not, but what I saw is undoubtedly small. In memory of this legend they perform the following ceremony. Twice a year water is brought from the sea to the temple. It is brought not by the priests only, but by all Syria and Arabia, ay and from beyond the Euphrates many men go to the sea, and all of them bring water. The water is poured into the chasm, and though the chasm is small, yet it receives a mighty

---

[1] *De dea Syria.* The modern scepticism as to the authorship of this treatise is purely arbitrary and rests on no better foundation than that uncritical criticism which aims, not so much at the discovery of truth, as at the display of the critic's acumen in doubting or denying what everybody else had believed before he was born, and what most sensible people will continue to believe long after he is dead.

deal of water. In doing this they say that they comply with the custom which Deucalion instituted in the sanctuary for a memorial at once of calamity and of mercy."[1] Moreover, at the north gate of the great temple there stood two tall columns, or rather obelisks, each about three hundred and sixty feet high ; and twice a year a man used to ascend one of them and remain for seven days in that airy situation on the top of the obelisk. Opinions differed as to why he went there, and what he did up aloft. Most people thought that at that great height he was within hail of the gods in heaven, who were near enough to hear distinctly the prayers which he offered on behalf of the whole land of Syria. Others, however, opined that he clambered up the obelisk to signify how men had ascended to the tops of mountains and of tall trees in order to escape from the waters of Deucalion's flood.[2]

In this late Greek version of the deluge legend the resemblances to the Babylonian version are sufficiently close ; and a still nearer trait is supplied by Plutarch, who says that Deucalion let loose a dove from the ark in order to judge by its flight or its return whether the storm still continued or had abated.[3] In this form the Greek legend of the great flood was unquestionably coloured, if not moulded, by Semitic influence, whether the colours and the forms were imported from Israel or from Babylon.

But Hierapolis, on the Euphrates, was not the only place in Western Asia which Greek tradition associated with the deluge of Deucalion. There was, we are told, a certain Nannacus, King of Phrygia, who lived before the time of Deucalion, and, foreseeing the coming catastrophe, gathered his people into the sanctuaries, there to weep and pray. Hence "the age of Nannacus" became a proverbial expression for great antiquity or loud lamentations.[4] According to another account, Nannacus (or Annacus), the Phrygian, lived over 300 years, and when his neighbours, apparently tired of the old man, inquired of the oracle how much longer he might be expected to live, they received the discouraging reply that when the patriarch died all men would perish with him. So the Phrygians lamented bitterly, which gave rise to the old proverb about "weeping for Nannacus."[5] The Greek satyric poet Herodas puts the proverb in the mouth of a mother who brings her brat to the schoolmaster to receive a richly deserved thrashing ; and in so doing she refers sorrowfully to the cruel necessity she was under of paying the school fees, even though she were to "weep like Nannacus."[6] When the Deluge

---

[1] Lucian, *De dea Syria*, 12 *sq.* In the opening words of this passage (οἱ μὲν ὦν πολλοὶ Δευκαλίωνα τὸν Σισύθεα τὸ ἱρὸν εἴσασθαι λέγουσι) the name Σισύθεα is an emendation of Buttmann's for the MS. reading Σκύθεα. See Ph. Buttmann, *Mythologus* (Berlin, 1828–9), i, 191 *sq.* If the emendation is correct the name Sisythes may be, as scholars suppose, a variant of Xisuthrus, the name of the hero in Berosus's Greek version of the flood legend. See above, p. 234 ; and H. Usener, *Die Sintfluthsagen*, pp. 47 *sq.*

[2] Lucian, *De dea Syria*, 28.   [3] Plutarch, *De sollertia animalium*, 13.

[4] Suidas, *s.v.* Νάννακος ; Zenobius, *Cent.*, vi, 10 ; Macarius, *Cent.*, ii, 23, viii, 4 ; Apostolius, *Cent.*, xv, 100.

[5] Stephanus Byzantius, *s.v.* Ἰκόνιον.   [6] Herodas, *Mimes*, iii, 10.

had swept away the whole race of mankind, and the earth had dried up again, Zeus commanded Prometheus and Athena to fashion images of mud, and then, summoning the winds, he bade them breathe into the mud images and make them live. So the place was called Iconium, after the images (*eikones*) which were made there.[1] Some have thought that the patriarchal Nannacus, or Annacus, was no other than the Biblical Enoch, or Hanoch,[2] who lived before the Flood for 365 years, and was then removed from the world in a mysterious fashion.[3] But against this identification it is to be said that the name Nannacus would seem to be genuine Greek, since it occurs in Greek inscriptions of the island of Cos.[4]

Another city of Asia Minor which appears to have boasted of its connexion with the Great Flood was Apamea Cibotos, in Phrygia. The surname of Cibotos, which the city assumed,[5] is the Greek word for chest, or ark; and on coins of the city, minted in the reigns of Severus, Macrinus, and Philip the Elder, we see the ark floating on water with two passengers in it, whose figures appear from the waist upwards; beside the ark two other human figures, one male and the other female, are represented standing; and lastly, on the top of the chest are perched two birds, one of them said to be a raven and the other a dove carrying an olive-branch. As if to remove all doubt as to the identification of the legend, the name Noe, the Greek equivalent of Noah, is inscribed on the ark. No doubt the two human figures represent Noah and his wife twice over, first in the ark, and afterwards outside of it.[6] These coin types prove unquestionably that in the third century of our era the people of Apamea were acquainted with the Hebrew tradition of the Noachian deluge in the form in which the story is narrated in the Book of Genesis. They may easily have learned it from their Jewish fellow-citizens, who in the first century before our era were so numerous or so wealthy that on one occasion they contributed no less than 100 pounds weight of gold to be sent as an offering to Jerusalem.[7] Whether at Apamea the tradition of the Deluge

---

[1] Stephanus Byzantius, *s.v.* Ἰκόνιον.

[2] חֲנוֹךְ

[3] Genesis v, 23 *sq.* The identification, first suggested by Ph. Buttmann (*Mythologus*, Berlin, 1828–9, i, 175 *sqq.*, 187 *sq.*), is accepted by E. Babelon. See E. Babelon, "La Tradition Phrygienne du Déluge," *Revue de l'Histoire des Religions*, xxiii (1891), p. 180. Buttmann even identified Aeacus, the righteous hero of Aegina, with Nannacus and Enoch.

[4] H. Collitz und F. Bechtel, *Sammlung der griechischen Dialekt-Inschriften*, iii, 1 (Göttingen, 1899), p. 342, Inscr. No. 3623 c, 51 ; G. Dittenberger, *Sylloge Inscriptionum Graecarum*² (Leipsic, 1898–1901), ii, p. 732, No. 885.

[5] Strabo, xi, 6, 3, and 8, 13, pp. 569, 576, ed. Casaubon ; Pliny, *Nat. Hist.*, v, 106. Adolphe Reinach preferred to suppose that the name is a native Asiatic word assimilated by popular etymology to a Greek one. He compared Kibyra, Kibyza, Kybistra, and Kybela. See his *Noé Sangariou* (Paris, 1913), pp. 38 *sq.*

[6] Barclay V. Head, *Historia Numorum* (Oxford, 1887), p. 558 ; E. Babelon, "La Tradition Phrygienne du Déluge," *Revue de l'Histoire des Religions*, xxiii (1891), pp. 180 *sq.*

[7] Cicero, *Pro Flacco*, 28. We know from Josephus (*Antiquit. Jud.*, xii, 3, 4) that Antiochus the Great issued orders for transplanting two thousand Jewish families from Mesopotamia and Babylonia to Lydia and Phrygia, and for settling them there as colonists on very liberal terms. This may well have been the origin of the Jewish settlement at Apamea, as E. Babelon has

was purely Jewish in origin, or whether it was grafted upon an old native legend of a great flood, is a question on which scholars are not agreed.[1]

Though the deluge associated with the name of Deucalion was the most familiar and famous, it was not the only one recorded by Greek tradition. Learned men, indeed, distinguished between three such great catastrophes which had befallen the world at different epochs. The first, we are told, took place in the time of Ogyges, the second in the time of Deucalion, and the third in the time of Dardanus.[2] Ogyges (or Ogygus, as the name is also spelled) is said to have founded and reigned over Thebes in Bœotia,[3] which, according to the learned Varro, was the oldest city in Greece, having been built in antediluvian times before the earliest of all the floods.[4] The connexion of Ogyges with Bœotia in general and with Thebes in particular is further vouched for by the name Ogygian which was bestowed on the land,[5] on the city,[6] and on one of its gates.[7] Yet the Athenians, jealous of the superior antiquity which this tradition assigned to their hated rival, claimed the ancient Bœotian hero as an aboriginal of their country[8]; one tradition describes Ogyges as a king of Attica,[9] and another represents him as the founder and king of Eleusis.[10] So great was the devastation wrought in Attica by the flood that the country remained without kings from the time of Ogyges down to the reign of Cecrops.[11] If we may trust the description of a rhetorical

pointed out ("La Tradition Phrygienne du Déluge," *Revue de l'Histoire des Religions*, xxiii (1891), pp. 177 *sq.*).

[1] The view that the flood legend of Apamea was purely Jewish, without any basis of local tradition, is maintained by E. Babelon ("La Tradition Phrygienne du Déluge," *Revue de l'Histoire des Religions*, xxiii (1891), pp. 174–83). On the other hand, the composite character of the Apamean legend was maintained by H. Usener (*Die Sintfluthsage*, pp. 48–50) and advocated, with a great array of learning, by Adolphe Reinach in his treatise, *Noé Sangariou* (Paris, 1913). I confess that the arguments adduced in favour of an aboriginal flood legend at Apamea appear to me to carry little weight, resting rather on a series of doubtful combinations than on any solid evidence.

[2] Nonnus, *Dionys.*, iii, 202-19 ; Scholiast on Plato, *Timaeus*, p. 22A. That the deluge of Ogyges was prior to the deluge of Deucalion is affirmed also by Augustine (*De Civitate Dei*, xviii, 8) and Servius (on Virgil, *Eclog.*, vi, 41), neither of whom, however, mention the deluge of Dardanus.

[3] Pausanias, ix, 5, 1 ; Servius, on Virgil, *Eclog.*, vi, 41, "*sub Ogyge, rege Thebanorum.*"

[4] Varro, *Rerum Rusticarum*, iii, 1.

[5] Strabo, ix, 2, 18, p. 407, ed. Casaubon ; Stephanus Byzantius, *s.v.* Βοιωτία.

[6] Pausanias, ix, 5, 1 ; Apollonius Rhodius, *Argonaut*, iii, 1178 ; Festus, *De verborum significatione, s.v.* "Ogygia," p. 179, ed. C. O. Müller.

[7] Euripides, *Phoenissae*, 1113 ; Pausanias, ix, 8, 5 ; Scholiast on Apollonius Rhodius, *Argonaut.*, iii, 1178.

[8] Africanus, quoted by Eusebius, *Praeparatio Evangelica*, x, 10, 4.

[9] Scholiast on Plato, *Timaeus*, p. 22A.

[10] Africanus, quoted by Eusebius, *Praeparatio Evangelica*, x, 10, 7 ; Eusebius, *Chronic.*, ed. A. Schoene, vol. ii, p. 17 ; Isidorus Hispalensis, *Origines*, xiii, 22, 3. Some said that the hero Eleusis, from whom the city took its name, was a son of Ogygus (Pausanias, i, 38, 7).

[11] Africanus, quoted by Eusebius, *Praeparatio Evangelica*, x, 10, 9. Among the authorities cited by Africanus (in Eusebius, *op. cit.*, x, 10, 5) are the Attic historians Hellanicus and Philochorus.

poet, the whole earth was submerged by the Deluge, even the lofty peaks of Thessaly were covered, and the snowy top of Parnassus itself was lashed by the snowy billows.[1]   With regard to the date of the catastrophe, some writers of antiquity profess to give us more or less exact information. The learned Roman scholar Varro tells us that the Bœotian Thebes was built about 2,100 years before the time when he was writing, which was in or about the year 36 B.C. ; and as the Deluge, according to him, took place in the lifetime of Ogyges, but after he had founded Thebes, we infer that in Varro's opinion the Great Flood occurred in or soon after the year 2136 B.C.[2]   Still more precise is the statement of Julius Africanus, a Christian author who drew up a chronicle of the world from the Creation down to the year 221 A.D. He affirms that the deluge of Ogyges happened just 1,020 years before the first Olympiad, from which the Greeks dated their exact reckoning; and as the first Olympiad fell in the year 776 B.C., we arrive at the year 1796 B.C. as the date to which the Christian chronicler referred the date of the great Ogygian flood. It happened, he tells us, in the reign of Phoroneus, king of Argos. He adds for our further information that Ogyges, who survived the deluge to which he gave his name, was a contemporary of Moses and flourished about the time when that great prophet led the children of Israel out of Egypt; and he clinches his chain of evidence by observing that at a time when God was visiting the land of Egypt with hailstorms and other plagues, it was perfectly natural that distant parts of the earth should simultaneously feel the effects of the divine anger, and in particular it was just and right that Attica should smart beneath the rod, since according to some people, including the historian Theopompus, the Athenians were in fact colonists from Egypt and therefore shared the guilt of the mother-country.[3]   According to the Church historian Eusebius, the great flood in the time of Ogyges occurred about one thousand two hundred years after the Noachian deluge and two hundred and fifty years before the similar catastrophe in the days of Deucalion.[4]   It would seem indeed to have been a point of honour with the early Christians to claim for the flood recorded in their sacred books an antiquity far more venerable than that of

---

[1] Nonnus, *Dionys*, iii, 206–8.

[2] Varro, *Rerum Rusticarum*, iii, 1, 3. In his preface to this treatise on agriculture (bk. i, ch. i) Varro indicates that it was written in his eightieth year ; and as he was born in 116 B.C., he must have been composing the work in question in or about 36 B.C. From Arnobius (*Adversus Gentes*, v, 8) we learn that Varro reckoned less than two thousand years from Deucalion's flood to the consulship of Hirtius and Pansa in 43 B.C., which seems to show that he dated Deucalion's flood fully a hundred years later than that of Ogyges. Compare the commentary of Meursius on Varro, printed in J. G. Schneider's edition of the *Scriptores Rei Rusticae Veteres Latini* (Leipsic, 1794–6), vol. i, part 2, p. 491.

[3] Julius Africanus, quoted by Eusebius, *Praeparatio Evangelica*, x, 10. That the deluge of Ogyges happened in the reign of Phoroneus, King of Argos, is mentioned also by the Christian writers, Tatian (*Oratio ad Graecos*, p. 150, ed. J. C. T. Otto) and Clement of Alexandria (*Strom.*, i, 21, § 102, p. 379, ed. Potter). Compare H. Fynes Clynton, *Fasti Hellenici*, i (Oxford, 1834), pp. 5–8.

[4] Eusebius, *Chronic.*, ed. A. Schoene, vol. i, col. 71.

any flood described in mere profane writings. We have seen that Julius Africanus depresses Ogyges from the age of Noah to that of Moses; and Isidore, the learned bishop of Seville at the beginning of the seventh century, heads his list of floods with the Noachian deluge, while the second and third places in order of time are assigned to the floods of Ogyges and Deucalion respectively; according to him, Ogyges was a contemporary of the patriarch Jacob, while Deucalion lived in the days of Moses. The bishop was, so far as I am aware, the first of many writers who have appealed to fossil shells imbedded in remote mountains as witnesses to the truth of the Noachian tradition.[1]

If Ogyges was originally, as seems probable, a Bœotian rather than an Attic hero, the story of the deluge in his time may well have been suggested by the vicissitudes of the Copaic Lake which formerly occupied a large part of Central Bœotia.[2] For, having no outlet above ground, the lake depended for its drainage entirely on subterranean passages or chasms which the water had hollowed out for itself in the course of ages through the limestone rock, and according as these passages were clogged or cleared the level of the lake rose or fell. In no lake, perhaps, have the annual changes been more regular and marked than in the Copaic; for while in winter it was a reedy mere, the haunt of thousands of wild fowl, in summer it was a more or less marshy plain, where cattle browsed and crops were sown and reaped. So well recognized were the vicissitudes of the seasons that places on the bank of the lake such as Orchomenus, Lebadea, and Copae, had summer roads and winter roads by which they communicated with each other, the winter roads following the sides of the hills, while the summer roads struck across the plain. With the setting in of the heavy autumn rains in November the lake began to rise and reached its greatest depth in February or March, by which time the mouths of the emissories were completely submerged and betrayed their existence only by swirls on the surface of the mere. Yet even then the lake presented to the eye anything but an unbroken sheet of water. Viewed from a height, such as the acropolis of Orchomenus, it appeared as an immense fen, of a vivid green colour, stretching away for miles and miles, over-grown with sedge, reeds, and canes, through which the river Cephisus or Melas might be seen sluggishly oozing, while here and there a gleam of sunlit water, especially towards the north-east corner of the mere, directed the eye to what looked like ponds in the vast green swamp. Bare grey mountains on the north and east, and the beautiful wooded slopes of Helicon on the south, bounded the fen. In spring the water began to sink. Isolated brown patches, where no reeds grew, were the first to show as islands in the mere; and as the season advanced they expanded more and more till they met. By the middle of summer great stretches, especially in the middle and at the edges, were bare. In the higher parts the fat alluvial soil left by the retiring waters was sown

[1] Isidorus Hispalensis, *Origines*, xiii, 22, "*cujus indicium hactenus videmus in lapidibus, quos in remotis montibus conchis et ostreis concretos, saepe etiam cavatos aquis visere solemus.*"

[2] Ed. Meyer, *Geschichte des Alterthums*, ii (Stuttgart, 1896), p. 194.

by the peasants and produced crops of corn, rice, and cotton; while the lower parts, overgrown by rank grass and weeds, were grazed by herds of cattle and swine. In the deepest places of all the water often stagnated the whole summer, though there were years when it retreated even from these, leaving behind it only a bog or perhaps a stretch of white clayey soil, perfectly dry, which the summer heat seamed with a network of minute cracks and fissures. By the end of August the greater part of the basin was generally dry, though the water did not reach its lowest point till October. At that time what had lately been a fen was only a great brown expanse, broken here and there by a patch of green marsh, where reeds and other water-plants grew. In November the lake began to fill again fast.

Such was the ordinary annual cycle of changes in the Copaic Lake in modern times, and we have no reason to suppose that it was essentially different in antiquity. But at all times the water of the lake has been liable to be raised above or depressed below its customary level by unusually heavy or scanty rainfall in winter or by the accidental clogging or opening of the chasms. As we read in ancient authors of drowned cities on the margin of the lake,[1] so a modern traveller tells of villagers forced to flee before the rising flood, and of vineyards and corn-fields seen under water.[2]

Among the dead cities of which the ruins are scattered in and around the wide plain which was once the Copaic Lake none is more remarkable or excites our curiosity more keenly than one which bears the modern name of Goulas or Gla. Its ancient name and history are alike unknown: even legend is silent on the subject. The extensive remains occupy the broad summit of a low rocky hill or tableland which rises abruptly on all sides from the dead flat of the surrounding country. When the lake was full, the place must have been an island, divided by about a mile of shallow and weedy water from the nearest point in the line of cliffs which formed the eastern shore of the lake. A fortification wall, solidly built of roughly squared blocks of stone, encircles the whole edge of the tableland, and is intersected by four gates flanked by towers of massive masonry. Within the fortress are the ruins of other structures, including the remains of a great palace constructed in the style, though not on the plan, of the prehistoric palaces of Mycenae and Tiryns. The fortress and palace of Gla would seem to have been erected in the Mycenaean age by a people akin in civilization, if not in race, to the builders of Tiryns and Mycenae, though

---

[1] Strabo, ix, 2,18, p. 407, ed. Casaubon ; Pausanias, ix, 24, 2.

[2] On the Copaic Lake in antiquity see the excellent account in Strabo, ix, 2, 16–18, pp. 406 *sq.* Compare Pausanias, ix, 24, 1 *sq.* For modern accounts of it see C. Neumann und J. Partsch, *Physikalische Geographie von Griechenland* (Breslau, 1885), pp. 244–7 ; and especially A. Philippson, "Der Kopais See in Griechenland und seine Umgebung," *Zeitschrift der Gesellschaft für Erdkunde zu Berlin*, xxix (1894), pp. 1–90. I have allowed myself to quote from the description of the lake in my commentary on Pausanias (vol. v, pp. 110 *sqq.*), where I have cited the modern literature on the subject.

less skilled in the science of military engineering; for the walls do not exhibit the enormous stones of Tiryns, and the gates are arranged on a plan far less formidable to an assailant than the gates of the two Argive citadels. The scanty remains of pottery and other domestic furniture on the plateau appear to indicate that it was occupied only for a short time, and the traces of fire on the palace point to the conclusion that its end was sudden and violent. Everything within the place bears the imprint of a single plan and a single period: there is no trace of an earlier or a later settlement. Created at a blow, it would seem to have perished at a blow and never to have been inhabited again. In its solitude and silence, remote from all human habitations, looking out from its grey old walls over the vast Copaic plain to the distant mountains which bound the horizon on all sides, this mysterious fortress is certainly one of the most impressive sights in Greece.[1]

Can it be that this ancient and forgotten town, once lapped on all sides by the waters of the Copaic Lake, was the home of the legendary Ogyges, and that he forsook it, perhaps in consequence of an inundation, to migrate to the higher and drier site which was afterwards known as Thebes? The hypothesis would go some way to explain the legends which gathered round his memory; but it is no more than a simple guess, and as such I venture to hazard it.

The theory which would explain the great flood of Ogyges by an extra-ordinary inundation of the Copaic Lake, is to some extent supported by an Arcadian parallel. We have seen that in Greek legend the third great deluge was associated with the name of Dardanus. Now, according to one account, Dardanus at first reigned as a king in Arcadia, but was driven out of the country by a great flood, which submerged the lowlands and rendered them for a long time unfit for cultivation. The inhabitants retreated to the mountains, and for a while made shift to live as best they might on such food as they could procure; but at last, concluding that the land left by the water was not sufficient to support them all, they resolved to part; some of them remained in the country with Dimas, son of Dardanus, for their king; while the rest emigrated under the leadership of Dardanus himself to the island of Samothrace.[2] According to a Greek tradition, which the Roman Varro accepted, the birthplace of Dardanus was Pheneus in north Arcadia.[3] The place is highly significant, for, if we except the Copaic area, no valley in Greece is known to have been from antiquity subject to inundations on so vast a scale and for such long periods as the valley of Pheneus.[4] The natural conditions in the two regions are substantially alike. Both are basins in a limestone country without any outflow above ground; both receive the rain water which pours into them from the surrounding mountains; both are drained by subterranean channels which the

---

[1] For a fuller account of the place I may refer the reader to my commentary on Pausanias (vol. v, pp. 120 *sqq.*).

[2] Dionysius Halicarnasensis, *Antiquitates Romanae*, i, 61.

[3] Servius, on Virgil, *Aen.*, iii, 167.

[4] C. Neumann und J. Partsch, *Physikalische Geographie von Griechenland*, p. 252.

water has worn or which earthquakes have opened through the rock ; and whenever these outlets are silted up or otherwise closed, what at other times is a plain becomes converted for the time being into a lake.   But with these substantial resemblances are combined some striking differences between the two landscapes.   For while the Copaic basin is a vast stretch of level ground little above sea level and bounded only by low cliffs or gentle slopes, the basin of Pheneus is a narrow upland valley closely shut in on every side by high frowning mountains, their upper slopes clothed with dark pine woods and their lofty summits capped with snow for many months of the year.   The river which drains the basin through an underground channel is the Ladon, the most romantically beautiful of all the rivers of Greece.   Milton's fancy dwelt on " sanded Ladon's lilied banks "; even the prosaic Pausanias exclaimed that there was no fairer river either in Greece or in foreign lands[1]; and among the memories which I brought back from Greece I recall none with more delight than those of the days I spent in tracing the river from its birthplace in the lovely lake, first to its springs on the far side of the mountain, and then down the deep wooded gorge through which it hurries, brawling and tumbling over rocks in sheets of greenish-white foam, to join the sacred Alpheus.   Now the passage by which the Ladon makes its way underground from the valley of Pheneus has been from time to time blocked by an earthquake, with the result that the river has ceased to flow. When I was at the springs of the Ladon in 1895, I learned from a peasant on the spot that three years before, after a violent shock of earthquake, the water ceased to run for three hours, the chasm at the bottom of the pool was exposed, and fish were seen lying on the dry ground.   After three hours the spring began to flow a little, and three days later there was a loud explosion, and the water burst forth in immense volume.   Similar stoppages of the river have been reported both in ancient and modern times ; and whenever the obstruction has been permanent the valley of Pheneus has been occupied by a lake varying in extent and depth in proportion to the more or less complete stoppage of the subterranean outlet.   According to Pliny there had been down to his day five changes in the condition of the valley from wet to dry and from dry to wet, all of them caused by earthquakes.[2]   In Plutarch's time the flood rose so high that the whole valley was under water, which pious folk attributed to the somewhat belated wrath of Apollo at Hercules, who had stolen the god's prophetic tripod from Delphi and carried it off to Pheneus about a thousand years before.[3]   However, later in the same century the waters had again subsided, for the Greek traveller Pausanias found the bottom of the valley to be dry land, and knew of the former existence of the lake only by tradition.   At the beginning of the nineteenth century the basin was a swampy plain, for the most part covered with fields of wheat or barley.   But shortly after the expulsion of the Turks, through neglect of the precautions which the Turkish governor had taken to keep

---

[1] Pausanias, viii, 25, 13.

[2] Pliny, *Nat. Hist.*, xxxi, 54.

[3] Plutarch, *De sera numinis vindicta*, 12.

the mouth of the subterranean outlet open, the channel became blocked, the water, no longer able to escape, rose in its bed, and by 1830 it formed a deep lake about five miles long by five miles wide. And a broad lake of greenish-blue water it was when I saw it in the autumn of 1895, with the pine-clad mountains descending steeply in rocky declivities or sheer precipices to the water's edge, except for a stretch of level ground on the north, where the luxuriant green of vineyards and maize-fields contrasted pleasingly with the blue of the lake and the sombre green of the pines. The whole scene presented rather the aspect of a Swiss than of a Greek landscape. A few years later and the scene was changed. Looking down into the valley from a pass on a July afternoon, a more recent traveller beheld, instead of an expanse of sea-blue water, a blaze of golden corn with here and there a white point of light showing where a fustanella'd reaper was at his peaceful toil. The lake had disappeared, perhaps for ever; for we are told that measures have now been taken to keep the subterranean outlets permanently open, and so to preserve for the corn the ground which has been won from the water.[1]

A permanent mark of the height to which the lake of Pheneus attained in former days and at which, to all appearance, it must have stood for many ages, is engraved on the sides of the mountains which enclose the basin. It is a sharply cut line running round the contour of the mountains at a uniform level of not less than a hundred and fifty feet above the bottom of the valley. The trees and shrubs extend down the steep slopes to this line and there stop abruptly. Below the line the rock is of a light-yellow colour and almost bare of vegetation; above the line the rock is of a much darker colour. The attention of travellers has been drawn to this conspicuous mark from antiquity to the present day. The ancient traveller Pausanias noticed it in the second century of our era, and he took it to indicate the line to which the lake rose at the time of its highest flood, when the city of Pheneus was submerged.[2] This interpretation has been questioned by some modern writers, but there seems to be little real doubt that the author of the oldest Greek guide-book was substantially right; except that the extremely sharp definition of the line, and its permanence for probably much more than two thousand years, appear to point to a long-continued persistence of the lake at this high level rather than to a mere sudden and temporary rise in a time of inundation. "It is evident," says the judicious traveller Dodwell, "that a temporary inundation could not effect so striking a difference in the superficies of the rock, the colour of which must have been changed from that of the upper parts by the concreting deposit of many ages."[3]

---

[1] C. Neumann und J. Partsch, *Physikalische Geographie von Griechenland*, pp. 252 *sq.*; A. Philippson, *Der Peloponnes* (Berlin, 1892), pp. 144–146 ; J. ff. Baker-Penoyre, " Pheneus and the Pheneatiké," *Journal of Hellenic Studies*, xxii (1902), pp. 228–240. For further details as to the lake and the river I may refer the reader to my commentary on Pausanias (vol. iv, pp. 230 *sqq.*, 262 *sq.*, 287 *sqq.*).

[2] Pausanias, viii, 14, 1.

[3] E. Dodwell, *Classical and Topographical Tour through Greece* (London, 1819), ii, 436. This is the view also of the latest writer on the subject, Mr. Baker-Penoyre. See his article,

In a valley which has thus suffered so many alternations between wet and dry, between a broad lake of sea-blue water and broad acres of yellow corn, the traditions of great floods cannot be lightly dismissed ; on the contrary, everything combines to confirm their probability. The story, therefore, that Dardanus, a native of Pheneus, was compelled to emigrate by a great inundation which swamped the lowlands, drowned the fields, and drove the inhabitants to the upper slopes of the mountains, may well rest on a solid foundation of fact. And the same may be true of the flood recorded by Pausanias, which rose and submerged the ancient city of Pheneus at the northern end of the lake.[1]

From his home in the highlands of Arcadia the emigrant Dardanus is said to have made his way to the island of Samothrace.[2] According to one account, he floated thither on a raft[3] ; but according to another version of the legend, the great flood overtook him, not in Arcadia, but in Samothrace, and he escaped on an inflated skin, drifting on the face of the waters till he landed on Mount Ida, where he founded Dardania, or Troy.[4] Certainly, the natives of Samothrace, who were great sticklers for their antiquity, claimed to have had a deluge of their own before any other nation on earth. They said that the sea rose and covered a great part of the flat land in their island, and that the survivors retreated to the lofty mountains which still render Samothrace one of the most conspicuous features in the northern Aegean, and are plainly visible in clear weather from Troy.[5] As the sea still pursued them in their retreat, they prayed to the gods to deliver them, and on being saved they set up landmarks of their salvation all round the island and built altars on which they continued to sacrifice down to later ages. And many centuries

---

"Pheneus and the Pheneatiké," *Journal of Hellenic Studies*, xxii (1902), pp. 231 *sqq.* The German geologist, Mr. A. Philippson, took the line to mark the level to which the lake rose in 1830 (*Der Peloponnes*, p. 146). But as the lake suddenly fell again in 1834, it seems hardly possible that a flood lasting for only a few years should have scored its record so deeply on the sides of the mountains. As to the water-line, see further Sir William Gell, *Narrative of a Journey in the Morea* (London, 1823), p. 374 ; W. M. Leake, *Travels in the Morea* (London, 1830), iii, 147 *sqq.* ; E. Pouillon Boblaye, *Recherches Géographiques sur les ruines de la Morée* (Paris, 1835), p. 153, note ² ; E. Curtius, *Peloponnesos* (Gotha, 1851), ii, 188 *sq.* ; W. G. Clark, *Peloponnesus* (London, 1858), pp. 317 *sq.* The height of the water-line has been variously estimated. Dodwell and Curtius put it at several hundreds of feet ; W. G. Clark guessed that it might be about fifty feet above the level of the lake when he saw it. I roughly estimated the line by the eye at 200 or 300 feet above the lake, the level of which was probably lower than at the time of W. G. Clark's visit. Mr. Baker-Penoyre's estimate of the height is 150 feet above the bottom of the valley.

[1] Pausanias, viii, 14, 1.

[2] Dionysius Halicarnasensis, *Antiquitates Romanae*, i, 61, 3.

[3] Scholiast on Plato, *Timaeus*, p. 22A.

[4] Lycophron, *Cassandra*, 72 *sqq.*, with the scholia of Tzetzes ; Scholia on Homer, *Iliad*, xx, 215 (p. 558, ed. Im. Bekker, Berlin, 1825).

[5] W. Smith, *Dictionary of Greek and Roman Geography*, ii, 901, *s.v.* "Samothrace." Seen from the neighbouring island of Imbros, the mighty mass of Samothrace rises from the sea like the side of a Norwegian mountain, which indeed it closely resembles when the clouds and mists hang low on it in winter. See Alan G. Ogilvie, "Notes on the Geography of Imbros," *The Geographical Journal,* xlviii (1916), p. 144

after the Great Flood fishermen still occasionally drew up in their nets the stone capitals of columns, which told of cities drowned in the depths of the sea. The causes which the Samothracians alleged for the inundation were very remarkable. The catastrophe happened, according to them, not through a heavy fall of rain, but through a sudden and extraordinary rising of the sea occasioned by the bursting of the barriers which till then had divided the Black Sea from the Mediterranean. At that time the enormous volume of water dammed up behind these barriers broke bounds, and cleaving for itself a passage through the opposing land created the straits which are now known as the Bosphorus and the Dardanelles, through which the waters of the Black Sea have ever since flowed into the Mediterranean. When the tremendous torrent first rushed through the new opening in the dam, it washed over a great part of the coast of Asia, as well as the flat lands of Samothrace.[1]

Now this Samothracian tradition is to some extent confirmed by modern geology. "At no very distant period," we are told, "the land of Asia Minor was continuous with that of Europe, across the present site of the Bosphorus, forming a barrier several hundred feet high, which dammed up the waters of the Black Sea. A vast extent of eastern Europe and of western central Asia thus became a huge reservoir, the lowest part of the lip of which was probably situated somewhat more than 200 feet above the sea level, along the present southern watershed of the Obi, which flows into the Arctic Ocean. Into this basin the largest rivers of Europe, such as the Danube and the Volga, and what were then great rivers of Asia, the Oxus and Jaxartes, with all the intermediate affluents, poured their waters. In addition, it received the overflow of Lake Balkash, then much larger, and, probably, that of the inland sea of Mongolia. At that time the level of the Sea of Aral stood at least 60 feet higher than it does at present. Instead of the separate Black, Caspian, and Aral seas, there was one vast Ponto-Aralian Mediterranean, which must have been prolonged into arms and fiords along the lower valleys of the Danube and the Volga (in the course of which Caspian shells are now found as far as the Kama), the Ural, and the other affluent rivers—while it seems to have sent its overflow northward, through the present basin of the Obi."[2] This enormous reservoir, or vast inland sea, pent in and held up by a high natural dam joining Asia Minor to the Balkan Peninsula, appears to have existed down to the Pleistocene Period; and the erosion of the Dardanelles, by which the pent-up waters at last found their way into the Mediterranean, is believed to have taken place towards the end of the Pleistocene Period or later.[3] But man is now known for certain to have inhabited Europe in the Pleistocene Period; some hold that he

---

[1] Diodorus Siculus, v, 47. Among the proofs of the great antiquity of the Samothracians, according to this historian, was their archaic dialect, of which many examples survived in their religious ritual down to his time.

[2] T. H. Huxley, "The Aryan Question," *Collected Essays,* vol. vii (London, 1906), pp. 300 *sq.*

[3] T. H. Huxley, "Hasisadra's Adventure," *Collected Essays,* vol. iv (London, 1911), pp. 275, 276.

inhabited it in the Pliocene or even the Miocene Period.[1]   Hence it seems possible that the inhabitants of Eastern Europe should have preserved a traditional memory of the vast inland Ponto-Aralian Sea, and of its partial desiccation through the piercing of the dam which divided it from the Mediterranean—in other words, through the opening of the Bosphorus and the Dardanelles.   If that were so, the Samothracian tradition might be allowed to contain a large element of historical truth in regard to the causes assigned for the catastrophe.   On the other hand geology seems to lend no support to the tradition of the catastrophe itself.   For the evidence tends to prove that the strait of the Dardanelles was not opened suddenly, like the bursting of a dam, either by the pressure of the water or the shock of an earthquake, but that on the contrary it was created gradually by a slow process of erosion which must have lasted for many centuries or even thousands of years; for the strait "is bounded by undisturbed Pleistocene strata forty feet thick, through which, to all appearances, the present passage has been quietly cut."[2]   Thus the lowering of the level of the Ponto-Aralian Sea to that of the Mediterranean can hardly have been sudden and catastrophic, accompanied by a vast inundation of the Asiatic and European coasts; more probably it was effected so slowly and gradually that the total amount accomplished in a generation would be imperceptible to ordinary observers, or even to close observers unprovided with instruments of precision.   Hence, instead of assuming that Samothracian tradition preserved a real memory of a widespread inundation consequent on the opening of the Dardanelles, it seems safer to suppose that this story of a great flood is nothing but the guess of some early philosopher, who rightly divined the origin of the straits without being able to picture to himself the extreme slowness of the process by which nature had excavated them.   As a matter of fact, the eminent physical philosopher Strabo, who succeeded Theophrastus as head of the Peripatetic School in 287 B.C., actually maintained this view on purely theoretical grounds, not alleging it as a tradition which had been handed down from antiquity, but arguing in its favour from his observations of the natural features of the Black Sea.   He pointed to the vast quantities of mud annually washed down by great rivers into the Euxine, and he inferred that but for the outlet of the

---

[1] Sir Charles Lyell, *The Student's Elements of Geology*, Third Edition (London, 1878), pp. 128 *sqq.*; A. de Quatrefages, *The Human Species* (London, 1879), pp. 142–53; Sir John Lubbock (Lord Avebury), *Prehistoric Times*, Fifth Edition (London and Edinburgh, 1890), pp. 422 *sqq.*; W. J. Sollas, *Ancient Hunters* (London, 1915), pp. 59–86.   None of these writers definitely assents to the view that man existed in the Pliocene or even Miocene Period. Sir John Lubbock (Lord Avebury) expresses himself doubtfully on the point.   Professor Sollas sums up his conclusion (p. 85) as follows : " We have seen that the order of succession in time of fossil remains of the Mammalia and especially of apes and men suggests that man, in the strictest sense, *Homo sapiens*, is a creature of Pleistocene time ; as we look backwards into the past we lose sight of him before the close of that age and encounter in his place forms specifically and even generically distinct ; that other species of the human family might have already come into existence in the Pliocene epoch seems possible, but scarcely in the Miocene, and still less in the Oligocene epoch."

[2] T. H. Huxley, "Hasisadra's Adventure." *Collected Essays*, vol. iv (London, 1911), p. 281.

Bosphorus the basin of that sea would in time be silted up. Further, he conjectured that in former times the same rivers had forced for themselves a passage through the Bosphorus, allowing their collected waters to escape first to the Propontis and then from it through the Dardanelles to the Mediterranean. Similarly he thought that the Mediterranean had been of old an inland sea, and that its junction with the Atlantic was effected by the dammed-up water cutting for itself an opening through the Straits of Gibraltar.[1] Accordingly we may conclude that the cause which the Samothracians alleged for the Great Flood was derived from an ingenious speculation rather than from an ancient tradition.

There are some grounds for thinking that the flood story which the Greeks associated with the names of Deucalion and Pyrrha may in like manner have been, not so much a reminiscence of a real event, as an inference founded on the observation of certain physical facts. We have seen that in one account the mountains of Thessaly are said to have been parted by the deluge in Deucalion's time, and that in another account the ark, with Deucalion in it, is reported to have drifted to Mount Othrys in Thessaly. These references seem to indicate Thessaly as the original seat of the legend; and the indication is greatly strengthened by the view which the ancients took of the causes that had moulded the natural features of the country. Thus Herodotus relates a tradition that in ancient times Thessaly was a great lake or inland sea, shut in on all sides by the lofty mountains of Ossa and Pelion, Olympus, Pindus, and Othrys, through which there was as yet no opening to allow the pent-up waters of the rivers to escape. Afterwards, according to the Thessalians, the sea-god Poseidon, who causes earthquakes, made an outlet for the lake through the mountains by cleaving the narrow gorge of Tempe, through which the River Peneus has ever since drained the Thessalian plain. The pious historian intimates his belief in the truth of this local tradition. " Whoever believes," says he, " that Poseidon shakes the earth, and that chasms caused by earthquakes are his handiwork, would say, on seeing the gorge of the Peneus, that Poseidon had made it. For the separation of the mountains, it seems to me, is certainly the effect of an earthquake."[2] The view of the father of history was substantially accepted by later writers of antiquity,[3] though one of them would attribute the creation of the gorge and the drainage of the lake to the hero Hercules, among whose beneficent labours for the good of mankind the construction of waterworks on a gigantic scale was commonly reckoned.[4] More cautious or more philosophical authors contented themselves with referring the origin of the defile to a simple earthquake, without expressing any opinion as to the god or hero who may have set the tremendous disturbance in motion.[5]

---

[1] Strabo, i, 3, 4, pp. 49–50, ed. Casaubon. Compare Sir Charles Lyell, *Principles of Geology*,[12] (London, 1875), i, 24 ; E. H. Bunbury, *History of Ancient Geography*[2] (London, 1883), i, 658 *sq*.

[2] Herodotus, vii, 129.

[3] Philostratus, *Imag.*, ii, 14.

[4] Diodorus Siculus, iv, 18, 6.

[5] Strabo, ix, 5, 2, p. 430, ed. Casaubon ; Seneca, *Natur. Quaest.*, vi, 25, 2.

Yet we need not wonder that popular opinion in this matter should incline to the theory of divine or heroic agency, for in truth the natural features of the pass of Tempe are well fitted to impress the mind with a religious awe, with a sense of vast primordial forces which by the gigantic scale of their operations present an overwhelming contrast to the puny labours of man. The traveller who descends at morning into the deep gorge from the west may see, far above him, the snows of Olympus flushed with a golden glow under the beams of the rising sun, but as he pursues the path downwards the summits of the mountains disappear from view, and he is confronted on either hand only by a stupendous wall of mighty precipices shooting up in prodigious grandeur and approaching each other in some places so near that they almost seem to meet, barely leaving room for the road and river at their foot, and for a strip of blue sky overhead. The cliffs on the side of Olympus, which the traveller has constantly before his eyes, since the road runs on the south or right bank of the river, are indeed the most magnificent and striking in Greece, and in rainy weather they are rendered still more impressive by the waterfalls that pour down their sides to swell the smooth and steady current of the stream. The grandeur of the scenery culminates about the middle of the pass, where an enormous crag rears its colossal form in air, its soaring summit crowned with the ruins of a Roman castle. Yet the sublimity of the landscape is tempered and softened by the richness and verdure of the vegetation. In some parts of the defile the cliffs recede sufficiently to leave little grassy flats at their foot, where thickets of evergreens—the laurel, the myrtle, the wild olive, the arbutus, the *Agnus castus*—are festooned with wild vines and ivy, and variegated with the crimson bloom of the oleander and the yellow gold of the jasmine and laburnum, while the air is perfumed by the luscious odours of masses of aromatic plants and flowers. Even in the narrowest places the river bank is overshadowed by spreading plane-trees, which stretch their roots and dip their pendent boughs into the stream, their dense foliage forming so thick a screen as almost to shut out the sun. The scarred and fissured fronts of the huge cliffs themselves are tufted with dwarf oaks and shrubs, wherever these can find a footing, their verdure contrasting vividly with the bare white face of the limestone rock; while occasional breaks in the mountain wall open up vistas of forests of great oaks and dark firs mantling the steep declivities. The overarching shade and soft luxuriance of the vegetation strike the traveller all the more by contrast if he comes to the glen in hot summer weather after toiling through the dusty, sultry plains of Thessaly, without a tree to protect him from the fierce rays of the southern sun, without a breeze to cool his brow, and with little variety of hill and dale to relieve the dull monotony of the landscape.[1] No wonder that speculation should have early busied itself with

---

[1] E. Dodwell, *Classical and Topographical Tour through Greece* (London, 1819), ii, 109 *sqq.;* Sir William Gell, *The Itinerary of Greece* (London, 1819), pp. 275 *sqq.;* W. M. Leake, *Travels in Northern Greece* (London, 1835), iii, 390 *sqq.;* C. Bursian, *Geographie von Griechenland* (Leipsic, 1862–72), i, 58 *sqq.;* Christopher Wordsworth, *Greece, Pictorial, Descriptive, and Historical*, New Edition revised by H. F. Tozer (London, 1882), pp. 295 *sqq.* For ancient

the origin of this grand and beautiful ravine, and that primitive religion and science alike should have ascribed it to some great primeval cataclysm, some sudden and tremendous outburst of volcanic energy, rather than to its true cause, the gradual and age-long erosion of water.[1]

Hence we may with some confidence conclude that the cleft in the Thessalian mountains, which is said to have been rent by Deucalion's flood, was no other than the gorge of Tempe. Indeed, without being very rash, we may perhaps go further and conjecture that the story of the flood itself was suggested by the desire to explain the origin of the deep and narrow defile. For once men had pictured to themselves a great lake dammed in by the circle of the Thessalian mountains, the thought would naturally occur to them, what a vast inundation must have followed the bursting of the dam, when the released water, rushing in a torrent through the newly opened sluice, swept over the subjacent lowlands carrying havoc and devastation in its train ! If there is any truth in this conjecture, the Thessalian story of Deucalion's flood and the Samothracian story of the flood of Dardanus stood exactly on the same footing : both were mere inferences drawn from the facts of physical geography : neither of them contained any reminiscences of actual events. In short, both were what Sir Edward Tylor has called myths of observation rather than historical traditions.[2] Thus they differ from the Semitic story of a great flood, which appears to embody, in an exaggerated form, the recollection of a real catastrophe which once laid a large part of the lower valley of the Euphrates under water. To sum up, the difference between the Semitic and the Greek traditions is the difference between a legend and a myth.

descriptions of Tempe, see Aelian, *Var. Hist.*, iii, 1 ; Livy, xliv, 6 ; Pliny, *Nat. Hist.*, iv, 31 ; Catullus, lxiv, 285 *sqq.* ; Ovid, *Metamorph.*, i, 568 *sqq.* Of these descriptions that of Aelian is the most copious and most warmly coloured. He dwells with particular delight on the luxuriance of the vegetation.

[1] "That Olympus and Ossa were torn asunder and the waters of the Thessalian basin poured forth, is a very ancient notion and an often-cited 'confirmation' of Deucalion's flood. It has not yet ceased to be in vogue, apparently because those who entertain it are not aware that modern geological investigation has conclusively proved that the gorge of the Peneus is as typical an example of a valley of erosion as any to be seen in Auvergne or in Colorado" (T. H. Huxley, "Hasisadra's Adventure," *Collected Essays*, vol. iv, pp. 281 *sq.*).

[2] (Sir) Edward B. Tylor, *Researches into the Early History of Mankind* (London, 1878), pp. 306 *sqq.*

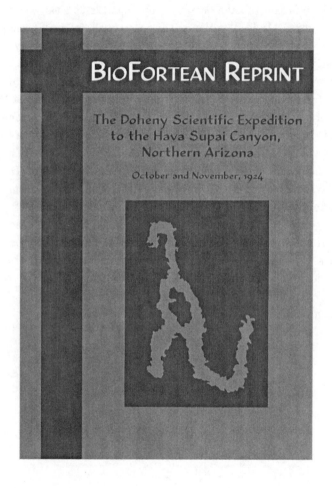

BioFortean Reprint

The Doheny Scientific Expedition
to the Hava Supai Canyon,
Northern Arizona

October and November, 1924

COACHWHIP PUBLICATIONS

COACHWHIPBOOKS.COM

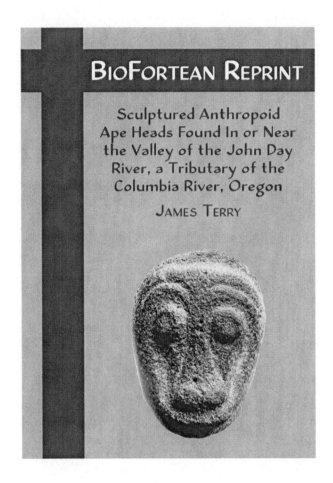

BioFortean Reprint

Sculptured Anthropoid Ape Heads Found In or Near the Valley of the John Day River, a Tributary of the Columbia River, Oregon

James Terry

Lightning Source UK Ltd.
Milton Keynes UK
UKOW03f2215300915

259569UK00004B/115/P